ALL OVER IT

HOW TO NAIL YOUR NEW PM JOB

Immediate actions for long-term success

DANIEL THOMASON

ISBN: 979-8-9942877-0-5 (paperback)

ISBN: 979-8-9942877-1-2 (e-book)

Library of Congress Control Number: 2026903977

mail@dthomason.com

To my wife Lena: lover, best friend, confidante, business partner, mother to my children, and generally incredible person. Life would be so much less without you.

To my amazing PM colleagues and mentors throughout the years: Tom, Antoine, Aida, Francesca, Gabi, Alex S, Dia, Annina, Amir, Mirela, Alex H, Paul, Paola, Nemanja, Andrew, Lindsey, Georgie, Dragan, Dean, Justin, Simona, Lea, Freddie, Lucrezia, Seb, Michael K, Giorgio, Kristina, Ahmed, Marek, Karen, Maria, Joonas, Triinu-Liis, Ilya, Maria, Gergő, Jörgen, Amul, Nick, Alya, Maggie, Fausto, Dong, Lisa, Robbie, Kevin, Annie, Eliška, Leyla, Garen, Eleanor, Stan, Kush, Stephen, Shonan, Hemen, Ryan, Atri, Alan, Pangu, Joris, Atef, Mark, Katherine, Steve, João, Niaz, Sumit, Gal, Michael H, Vivi, Vishal, Aurelia, Veronica, Kunal, Rohey, Fernanda, Nabila, Su Mei, Sid, Bhoomi, Cassie. This book is the product (ha!) of countless conversations and interactions with all of you; thank you.

CONTENTS

Impact   115

Future success   137

Conclusion   165

INTRODUCTION

WHY DOES THIS BOOK EXIST?

This is the book I wish I had when I was starting my PM career. I made lots of mistakes starting out: getting stuck into new projects too early in a new role, not staying in touch with key stakeholders, allowing my calendar to get filled with other people's priorities. And I learned from all of these mistakes, but they were painful lessons, and I wish I could have taken a shortcut to the resulting wisdom. This book is my attempt to help you with that, since it's too late for past Daniel.

My goal with this book is to give you a guide to the techniques and frameworks it took me years to learn and develop, and to help you position yourself to create value quickly.

There are other books out there that try to teach a generic strategy for starting a new job. While there is some value to be gained there, each job is sufficiently different in its demands and what it will take to onboard effectively that having a specialized approach is important.

There are also plenty of books that teach various aspects of the general craft and science of product management – I've referenced many in this book – and you should definitely consult those too. This book is much more focused on the specifics of the first few months of a new PM job: what you should do and when. Use other resources to supplement your knowledge about PM activities.

The other distinct approach that this book takes is the timeframe. There are many books and blog posts that teach you how to be successful in the first three months, or 30 days, or 1 week, or 60 seconds. And while that's well and good if you are in a hurry and can't wait, my view is that the minimum length of time to really be successful in a new job is 12 months. By that point you should have plenty to show for yourself, but you should also be well positioned to have even more impact going forward. Most importantly, you shouldn't already be feeling burnt out at all – something that is a high risk if you follow the much shorter timeframe recommended by other texts.

GOALS FOR THIS BOOK

1. Establish you as the **expert** in your domain

2. Help you build an effective **network** for getting things done

3. Start creating positive **impact** and build momentum to increase this over time

WHO IS THIS BOOK FOR?

This book is meant for people starting a new PM job. By "new" I don't necessarily mean that this is your first ever PM job, although this book will certainly be helpful if that's the case! I mean simply that you are starting a new job in a PM role. Whether that's a transfer from another role within the same company or a totally new company, this book is for you.

The target is individual contributor PMs; if you are starting a new job where your main responsibility is managing PMs, your work will look very different, and other resources will serve you better. These days there are a lot of hybrid manager/individual contributor (IC) positions in which you are managing other PMs but also still managing a product yourself – if that's you, then this book will be useful.

This book should be useful for every company size, from startup through to giant corporation, but it will be typically most helpful if you are in a for-profit company of at least 100 people.

First-time PMs will find most of the material in this book to be entirely new, but more experienced PMs should get plenty of value too: There will be many sections with novel ideas, and the rest should be at least a good refresher and provide concrete exercises to follow for a familiar topic.

I also assume that you have found a company you like, such that you want to grow your career there for at least a few years. If you find yourself unsure about that, you have a different, more urgent problem to solve.

HOW TO READ AND USE THIS BOOK

This is a practical book; you should judge its value not on whether it presents interesting ideas or whether it is nicely formatted (although hopefully it ticks both of these boxes too!), but by whether it improves your work life.

The book is designed to be a series of activities that will last across approximately the first 24 weeks of a new PM's time at a company. You should be getting constant value from the book, rather than it all being delivered in a big bang right at the end. Indeed, that's the whole point!

The action items are meant to complement and accentuate the regular day-to-day work of a PM; the book assumes that you'll already be doing all of the standard PM tasks like defining requirements, attending team meetings, and doing what needs to be done to launch new features. The risk that the book will help you mitigate is that *these tasks can easily fill your entire schedule as a new PM, but they are not sufficient for success.* By following this book, you'll also be investing in becoming more productive today and in the future.

The book roughly follows a chronological order of what I think your first 24 weeks should look like, but feel free to disregard that and dip in and out of sections that you feel are most valuable.

HABITS AND ROUTINES

"Where your ~~treasure~~ time is, there your heart will be also." Wise words for PMs to bear in mind. Your time is your most precious resource, the universal currency you convert into various kinds of value. The foundation for effective time management is how you allocate your time in a normal week – that is, where do you spend your time by default? These habits and routines will be the cornerstone of your work, so getting them right from the start will set you up for success.

MAKE TIME FOR IMPORTANT BUT NON-URGENT WORK

▶ **Timing**

○ Week 1, then revisit in week 5 and week 14 (once your Platonic ideal routine has been disrupted by messy reality)

▶ **Goal of chapter**

○ Help you to be proactive about where you want to spend your time to be most effective, and block your calendar to make this possible

▶ **Background: Why is this needed?**

○ The default use of your time will be putting out whichever fire is burning most aggressively at a given moment, and if you allow this to persist you will never get to higher-leverage work (like preventing fires from starting in the first place!). Advance thought and pre-commitments for time use are needed.

▶ **Resources**

○ *The 7 Habits of Highly Effective People* by Stephen Covey

○ *Deep Work: Rules for Focused Success in a Distracted World* by Cal Newport

○ *Make Time: How to Focus on What Matters Every Day* by Jake Knapp and John Zeratsky

○ Deep work slots: How to stay focused and avoid distractions (QR1)

○ What is the Eisenhower Matrix? A Guide for Product Managers (QR2)

○ The Eisenhower Matrix in Product Management (QR3)

○ 10 Ways to Handle Non-Urgent but Important Tasks (QR4)

○ The Eisenhower Matrix: Introduction and 3-Minute Video Tutorial (QR5)

QR1

QR2

QR3

QR4

QR5

I learned about this way of classifying activities from *The 7 Habits of Highly Effective People*, but it is also referred to as the Eisenhower Matrix, after the former U.S. President.

You can think of different tasks as existing along two axes: important vs not important, and urgent vs not urgent. These combine to make four quadrants.

Quadrant 1 is for tasks that are urgent and important: things like an impending executive review, or a feature launch. Quadrant 2 is important but not urgent: writing documentation, or playing around with competitors' products. Quadrant 3 is urgent but not important: the ding of a notification on your phone. And Quadrant 4 is neither urgent nor important: rearranging the knick knacks on your desk.

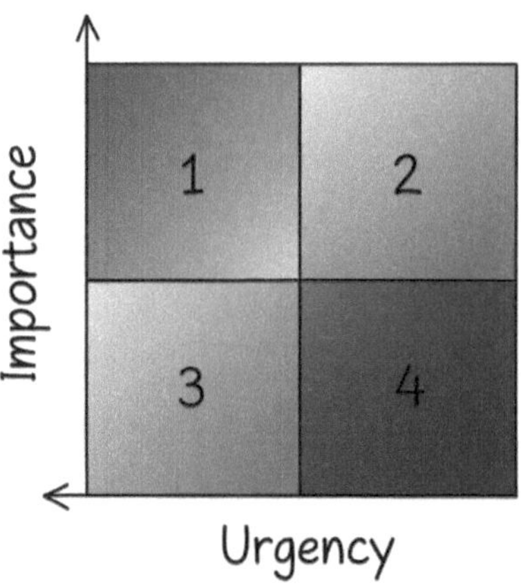

As a PM, you're going to be constantly dragged into Quadrants 1 and 3, because grease usually accrues to the squeakiest wheels. Your goals are (a) to spend enough time in Quadrant 2, because this is where the real value is created, and (b) to resist Quadrant 3 as much as possible. I guarantee that if you don't consciously and deliberately make time for Quadrant 2 activities, you will never get to them.

Examples of Quadrant 2 activities:

▶ Talking to users

▶ Reading about trends in your industry

▶ Just sitting and thinking

- ▶ Digging into the data
- ▶ Getting advice from other PMs
- ▶ Using your product

Shultz hour for just sitting and thinking

One particularly useful Quadrant 2 activity I picked up from an outstanding engineering manager I worked with (Hi Mike!) is the Shultz hour. This is named after George Shultz, a former U.S. Secretary of State. He had a permanent weekly one-hour block on his calendar, during which time he instructed his assistant that only two people could interrupt him: his wife, or the President. He used this time to think about bigger-picture things and zoom out from the minutiae that dominate everyday life. I highly recommend the same ritual for PMs, because it's very easy to get so caught up in the day-to-day work of unblocking launches or communicating with stakeholders or polishing that PRD that you forget to step back and *think* occasionally. Some of my best ideas have come out of blocking an hour like this. You can think about where your product fits into the wider company and industry, about *why* your customers use your product, about what you would do if your team suddenly doubled, etc. The cumulative effect of doing it regularly is that you'll have a nice clear picture of what's around you. No myopia here!

Action items

- ☐ Make your list of Quadrant 2 activities and how often you would ideally like to do them.

- ☐ Think back over your last year and mentally note which activities fit Quadrants 3 and 4. Consider how you could better avoid them going forward.

- ☐ Ask your manager what they think the highest-leverage activities are for your role.

CONTROL YOUR CALENDAR

▶ **Timing**

○ Week 1, then revisit in week 5 and week 14 (once your Platonic ideal routine has been disrupted by messy reality)

○ Should only take up to a day of effort each time

▶ **Goal of chapter**

○ Help you define how you want to spend your time to be maximally effective, and to shape your calendar around this so that you stand a chance of approximating the ideal

▶ **Background: Why is this needed?**

○ As a PM, you are at the nexus of a hive of activity and information. This means people will constantly want and need things from you, and if you let your time be taken up by whatever is demanded of you, you will end up running in place a lot and risk making minimal progress on your own priorities.

○ Put another way, your time is your most precious resource, so you should be budgeting and spending it carefully.

○ As with everything, going in with a clear vision of what a good outcome looks like is vital for getting there, and for recalibrating when your schedule inevitably gets messy.

▶ **Resources**

○ *Make Time: How to Focus on What Matters Every Day* by Jake Knapp and John Zeratsky

○ 7 Tips to Start Time Blocking Today **(QR1)**

○ Practical Product Management: Calendar Management **(QR2)**

○ How do the best product people manage their time? **(QR3)**

○ Calendar management tips: Tips to help take back your time **(QR4)**

QR1

QR2

QR3

QR4

Ground zero in this pursuit is, of course, your calendar. Your calendar should be the first tab you open in the morning and the last thing you look at each evening.

Critically, your calendar is not just an informative tool, telling you *what is happening* to you; it should be a proactive tool for you to allocate your time where you want to spend it.

Start with a list of activities you want to make sure you spend time on. The activities are likely to be very high-level (e.g. "look at product data", or "review customer support calls"), and that's fine – you'll be able to figure out exactly what to do in the moment. The point is to explicitly note down your high-value activities, particularly those that are likely to get drowned out by other noise – the Quadrant 2 activities.

Note: Your personal wellbeing is definitely an important Quadrant 2 item! This means setting reasonable working hours, allowing time for breaks, and setting an intensity cadence that works for you. Consider also blocking an hour to hit the gym in the middle of the day, if that works for you – nothing like a burst of exercise and a shower to refresh your brain!

Some specific tips that work for me:

▶ Put in recurring time blocks to make sure (or at least increase the likelihood) that you spend time on the things you know to be important but tend to forget in the heat of battle. I have them for catching up on my reading list, analyzing product data, and planning the week. "Focus time" in Google Calendar works well for this.

▶ Put in a recurring lunch block; be willing to sacrifice it if necessary but if you don't have it you will regularly be booked through lunch. This is especially important if you work with people in different time zones.

▶ Be very paranoid about recurring meetings – this is what will kill you. Every few months you should aggressively prune recurring meetings back: eliminate if you can (replacing them with a written update can work well), shorten them, or reduce their frequency.

▶ Politely resist people throwing one-off meetings on your calendar, especially if they don't have a clear purpose. My favorite tactic here is to message them to say, "Hey, not sure I can meet at that time but I can definitely respond quickly either here or via email if you have some questions."

▶ Communicate your working hours (Google Calendar lets you set this), and if you want to be super explicit, put blocks in your calendar for times when you absolutely *will not* work.

A few more thoughts on meetings. Meetings just for gleaning information are inefficient (although sometimes you have to force the issue if you don't get a response other ways, more on that later). Meetings should be used for either creating information (brainstorming), driving a decision, or for situations in which sharing the information will then immediately generate follow-up questions or responses (and hence to condense the feedback loop it's easier to do it live).

Action Items

☐ Put blocks on your calendar for the recurring habits you want to make time for

☐ Set your working hours, either in the calendar settings or by putting blocks in non-working hours

☐ Put a block for lunch

☐ Pick a day that you want to be meeting-free (or at least meeting-light!) and put a block for the whole day with a short explanatory note saying this is your day for thinking and catching up

I like Friday for this, helps me start the next week with a moderately clean slate!

SET UP A SYSTEM FOR CLOSING THE LOOP

▶ **Timing**

- Week 2, after you have generated enough information and tasks to have a sense of how they flow

▶ **Goal of chapter**

- Define how you will create a system you can 100% rely on to capture everything you need and resurface it at the right time, so that you can use your brain for better activities (and relax more!)

▶ **Background: Why is this needed?**

- I know a lot of anxious PMs, and the root cause is invariably the same: They constantly feel like there are things they should be doing that they have either forgotten or are letting slip. The latter is a prioritization problem combined with becoming comfortable with the never-done nature of the job, but the former is solvable through creating a watertight system for capturing tasks.

▶ **Resources**

- *Getting Things Done* by David Allen
- Building a Second Brain (QR1)

QR1

This is the TL;DR of the Getting Things Done system: Your brain is great at generating ideas and terrible at storing them, so get things out of your head and into a system. Being a PM is a cognitively demanding job – you are constantly required to make difficult prioritization decisions and context switch. As such, your biggest enemy is unnecessary cognitive burden, so you should have processes in place to fight this.

Your system needs to be simple! I've seen a lot of PMs with elaborate tagging and filing systems (their email client has 20+ colors in the sidebar), but they end up spending more time maintaining the system than they save. You just need the basics: a couple of places where you capture tasks and thoughts, a central place to store them, and a routine for putting time on your calendar to actually get the tasks done. This could be Google Keep, or Asana, or a running document, or even Post-its on your desk (although the risk of going analog is that they are then stuck in one location rather than going wherever your laptop goes!). But the important part is not the tool but the *system* – just pick something and run with it.

At the end of each day, set aside some time to close open loops: record action items you haven't got to, close as many tabs as you can, and ideally get to inbox zero (see above). I'm serious about closing tabs. They will weigh on your mind and raise your stress levels. Close them! Chrome has two amazing features for this: Reading List lets you dump things into a list for later consumption, and Tab Groups let you at least hide the problem.

At the end of each week, write a summary of what you did that week and look ahead to the following week to plan your calendar.

Consider sharing it with your manager – see *Use your manager effectively*.

Action items

- [ ] Write a short description of how you'll make sure you never miss a task

TAKE NOTES

▶ **Timing**

○ Week 1

▶ **Goal of chapter**

○ Figure out which types of notes you want to take, where you will store them, and which strategies you'll use to help yourself find them when you need them again in the future

▶ **Background: Why is this needed?**

○ Effective note-taking is a superpower – it stops information rot in its tracks, and multiplies the effective size of your brain many-fold. Starting your new PM job with a clear sense of which types of notes you want to take and what good notes look like will set you up for success here. Whoever takes/distributes the notes controls the narrative of the meeting, and ideally that's you!

▶ **Resources**

○ *How to Take Smart Notes: One Simple Technique to Boost Writing, Learning and Thinking* by Sönke Ahrens

○ Unlock a More Efficient Method to Note-Taking in Meetings as a Product Manager **(QR1)**

○ A Quick Guide to Meeting Notes for Managers **(QR2)**

○ Personal knowledge management guide **(QR3)**

○ Recovering the Lost Art of Note Taking **(QR4)**

○ How to take effective meeting notes: Templates and tips **(QR5)**

QR1

QR2

QR3

QR4

QR5

Most people's brains are very good at what is perhaps best described as vibes-based recollection. That is, you can recall the general gist of something you read or heard and connect it to other related ideas or knowledge, but you're unlikely to have an accurate memory of the details. For better fidelity, you need a medium other than your brain: enter note-taking. Note-taking also has a second benefit, though, which is to help with the vibe-based encoding in your brain by forcing you to think about it more consciously.

Bearing in mind the goal of notes (accurate record of details + aid in embedding something in your conceptual web), here are some note types you'll want to have:

- Meeting notes

- Summaries of long and/or important documents

- List of ideas for your product

- Map of who's who at the company – see *Map influence and information webs*.

- Unanswered questions

- Myriad other reasons!

    - Remember ABC: Always Be Capturing (notes). Or maybe that should be ABD: Always Be Documenting?

What does it look like to take good notes?

A common failure state for note-taking is to act like a stenographer, trying to capture every single thing. In the modern age of fairly accurate automatic transcripts, this is of limited value and – worse – fails the signal-to-noise test.

(A quick primer on that concept: *Signal* is the useful part of the input you receive, whereas *noise* is the random distraction. The terms come from information theory; ask Gemini about it! Increasing the signal-to-noise ratio means a given communication contains more of what is valuable and less useless filler.)

The goal with note-taking is to provide a record that *serves whatever purpose it is intended for*. Once again with feeling: *Notes need to serve a purpose* and, depending on that purpose, will look quite different.

If the purpose of the notes is to act as a summary for people who couldn't attend the meeting, then the notes should be fairly comprehensive. Note down what was discussed, who brought up each point, decisions made, and action items.

This was a useful task for a human a couple of years ago, but in the age of very accurate AI tools it no longer is. Just get a transcription tool.

If the purpose of the notes is as a persistent record for later reference in case of faulty memory or controversy, then they can be much sparser and just touch on the critical points. For example, if you and a PM from another team hash out a division of responsibilities for a project during a 1:1, writing the details of the split in a shared document or email is a good idea, but you can probably skip recording a lot of the discussion that got you there.

These should be rare. Shared notes are typically far more useful than private notes!

If the purpose of the notes is solely for your own consumption later to jog your memory or help you make connections between ideas and information, then ask yourself: What will I want to remember later, and *how would I search for this if I vaguely remember it*? That second point is vital, since we are now in the era of search-first information retrieval (rather than location-first, as with a filing system). You will thank yourself for littering your notes with synonyms for what you're talking about, even if at the time you think, "Oh there is no chance I will ever forget about the discombobulation matrix reflux!" You're busy, and maybe in 3 months' time all you will remember is that it had something to do with wires. Putting the word "wires" in your notes will vastly increase the chance that you'll then find them when you need them.

This is a skill that improves with repetition and frustrating failure, so don't despair the first time you inevitably have to spend half an hour searching for a document. Just learn from the experience!

Closing the loop on the note lifecycle

After you've taken notes, consider the following step in their lifecycle. Some notes are for cold storage, meant to be there if and when you need them and otherwise content to just sit idle. Others will go stale if they're not reviewed and updated – maybe schedule time to do so. And still others have a definite date or timespan in which they will become important – put a note on your calendar or send an email to yourself and snooze it until the day you need it.

Action items

- ☐ Read up about some different note-taking methodologies (e.g. Cornell notes, Zettelkasten, bullet journalling) to see if any resonate with you and pick up some tips and tricks for your own notes

- ☐ Plan where you are going to store different note types

- ☐ Create templates for the one to three most common note types you will use and bookmark them for quick retrieval

- ☐ Schedule time every quarter for note system maintenance

MANAGE INFORMATION FLOW

▶ **Timing**

○ Week 2

○ Set up once, use forever

▶ **Goal of chapter**

○ Set up a structure and process around gathering information and connecting it to what you already know

▶ **Background: Why is this needed?**

○ Information is your lifeblood as a PM; without it you will make bad decisions and also find it hard to get anything done

▶ **Resources**

○ Knowledge Sharing Best Practices for Product Teams (QR1)

○ How to pick the most effective communication channels at work (QR2)

QR1

QR2

Information is your lifeblood as a PM; without it you will make bad decisions and also find it hard to get anything done. Consciously creating and optimizing a system for information flow is a very high-leverage activity.

Examples of information you need:

▶ Who is working on what?

▶ What's important to different people?

▶ Whose opinion carries weight in which circles?

▶ What are competitors doing?

▶ What is important to your users/partners/clients?

▶ How does upper management view your product/team?

▶ Have we tried this before?

▶ Are there other teams working on something similar?

These are not static but continually changing: You need a constant stream of this input. But this will become overwhelming unless you have a system to deal with it.

Your goal is to maximize the amount of useful information you get, subject to keeping the signal-to-noise ratio (see *Take Notes* for a quick explanation of this idea) above a fairly high threshold.

Two examples of the extremes you want to avoid:

1. Only talking to your boss and no-one else will result in a very high signal-to-noise ratio but a low amount of total information.

2. Reading every random document you find on the company Google Drive will probably unearth a lot of good nuggets but at the cost of sifting through a lot of dross – something you don't have time for.

When you first start, you won't know what you don't know, so the goal is to go wide to quickly triangulate which topics you need to keep investigating and which sources are high-signal. Use the snowball technique: Ask every person you meet if they could share any documents that would be useful to read and give you the names of some more people to meet (see *Meet key partners* for more on the latter). You don't want to seem demanding when you do this, so phrase it as a broad request: "Is there anything you would recommend I read? I'm eager to learn, so anything you can think of would be great!" This is sufficiently open-ended that you'll sometimes turn up unexpected gems.

Action items

- ☐ Create a document to store a list of things people have recommended you read, with space for your annotations

- ☐ Create a scratch document for dumping notes on the fly

- ☐ Block time in your calendar every two to four weeks to process, clean up, and review your notes

GET ACCESS TO WHAT YOU NEED

▶ **Timing**

○ Week 2

○ Takes a couple of days

○ Should only be needed once

▶ **Goal of chapter**

○ Get access to all the tools, data and documents you need to do your job, and do so nice and early so that you have it all ready when you are too busy to worry about this

▶ **Background: Why is this needed?**

○ One of the first things you need to do is make sure that the information and tools you need to do your job are at least available to you when you are ready to pick them up – this is surprisingly hard at many companies!

▶ **Resources**

○ This is very specific to your company, so ask your manager for resources here!

As a PM, you're expected to either have the answers or be able to find the answers to a very wide range of questions at extremely short notice. From "What does the login screen look like?" to "How many users actually click this button?" to "How much money did we make from feature X last year?", you're expected to be across it all.

High-quality, up-to-date documentation is the best possible way to be prepared for this (see *Document something misunderstood*), but there is a bootstrapping problem there – you can't document what you don't know. So the first task is to be able to find the required information when questions arise, either from your own investigations or from others'. And for that, the biggest barrier is *access* – to data, tools, current designs, test versions of your product, etc.

Getting access can also take a long time if you're working for a company in the awkward teenage years of "too big to ignore access controls completely but too young to have streamlined the process," or if you're working for a very old-school company where bureaucracy rules the roost (although if this is you, maybe you want to contemplate whether you're in the right job). So it's worth starting this journey early, long before you have a pressing need for something.

Examples of what you might need access to:

▶ Project management software, as an admin for your projects

  ○ This is crucial; I guarantee you will be sad at some point if you are dependent on someone else to make changes

▶ Figma files

▶ Data analytics software

  ○ Plus whatever logs, tables, dashboards are relevant to your product. This is likely to be one of the hardest things to get access to, so start early.

▶ Relevant documents/decks

  ○ Start with the most recent planning document and snowball from there

▶ Any other internal systems that you'll need to do your job

  ○ Find a PM who has been at the company a while and ask them which software they use at least weekly

▶ Access to a test environment so you can safely mess around with your product

> **Computer setup**
>
> Spend a couple of hours in your first week getting your computer set up the way you like it. You'll never have the luxury of this much free time again, so if you don't do this now you're likely to never get the chance again. If you don't have a preferred setup, you might want to put some thought into that: first we shape our tools, then our tools shape us, after all!
>
> If this is your first PM job, it's understandable if you don't necessarily have a preferred setup. My observation is that most other jobs have a lot more slack built into their schedules, which means that a suboptimal setup doesn't really bite you because you have plenty of time to work around it – likely you won't even notice. But as a PM there are never enough hours in the day, so any tiny irritations in your workflow will cause disproportionate problems.

Treat getting access to things as a forecasting game, where you are trying to guess what you'll need before you acutely need it. It only takes one experience of having an email from a VP that you can't answer because you don't have access to some critical bit of information or data to make you never want to be caught short again. Easy rule of thumb: When in doubt, request access (thanks to Ben M for that tip!).

The secret here – and with PM work in general – is to be regularly checking the horizon for what's next. A lot of PMs fall into the completely understandable but still bad habit of focusing so hard on execution of the current work that they miss potholes that would have been trivially easy to avoid had they looked up a bit earlier. More on this in the Impact section.

Action items

- [ ] Set up your computer for optimal productivity

    - [ ] Bonus: Ask some engineers for any setup tips they have, and try one or two

- [ ] Request access to the logs for your product

- [ ] Request access to the one to three most important tools for your role

RELATIONSHIPS

As a Product Manager, you get things done mainly via other people. You are a conduit, taking in information about what's important – to the company, to users, to partners, to other teams – and outputting clarity about where effort should be directed. This is all made possible by your network of relationships. There is a reason that this chapter is so early in the book: Building and tending relationships is one of the critical skills of an effective PM.

While you're just starting a new PM job, a shallow breadth-first search will serve you best. Then after you've established yourself, you want a two-tier approach: Key relationships getting regular quality time, and a wide web of people getting periodic check-ins.

GET TO KNOW YOUR ENGINEERING AND DESIGN COUNTERPARTS

▶ **Timing**

- ○ Week 2

▶ **Goal of chapter**

- ○ Get a handle on how to set up two of your most important relationships for success

▶ **Background: Why is this needed?**

- ○ The product triad – engineer, PM, and designer – is your holy trinity. Those other two functions are critical to the success of the product. These relationships will make or break you!

▶ **Resources**

- ○ The PM and design relationship – and how not to f**k it up (QR1)
- ○ Core Concept: The Product Trio (QR2)
- ○ Strength through tension – in defence of the product triad (QR3)
- ○ How we develop great PM/Engineering relationships at Asana (QR4)

QR1

QR2

QR3

QR4

Your engineering and design counterparts (i.e. the tech lead and/or engineering manager, and the designer you work with) need to be your closest allies in the company. If this isn't the case, you're in trouble from the start. Good, trusting relationships here will set you up for intelligent risk-taking and allocating your time to the best possible uses. But conflict will tear you and your team to shreds.

Building good products is a team sport, and if you don't work well with your teammates then you're in trouble. This is so important that if you really can't find a way to collaborate effectively with the engineering lead or designer, you should consider asking to change teams – that's how much this will hurt you.

> Sorry if I sound a bit hyperbolic here, but I will die on this hill.

But no more negativity – it's very likely that you'll have receptive, collaborative people to work with, and your main question will be how to best build those relationships.

Your starting point is to set up a regular 1:1 with each of them. I recommend fortnightly, but if things move especially fast at your company you might consider weekly. There are two goals at these meetings:

1. Exchange information about what's going on in the team and figure out open questions and how to tackle shared problems

2. Build mutual trust and respect

Goal 2 is the less obvious but far more important one, long term. That trust battery (see *Build credibility* for more on this) is what will let you get through moments of friction and tension without things blowing up. It makes each of you comfortable relying on the other in situations where you can't be present – something that will be happening all the time. For example, a PM might have to give a guess about engineering scope, or a designer might need to make a tentative product commitment. If both sides trust the other to be acting in good faith and in the best interests of the team, everything operates far more smoothly.

Apart from a good 1:1 cadence, you also want to liberally share information with your engineering and design partners. Add them to email threads in cc to keep them in the loop, send them useful docs or decks, and invite them to meetings where decisions are being made. The more like a partnership of equals you try to make this, the more they are likely to do the same.

This goes especially for planning. That's when these relationships can often sour, in my experience. PMs get caught up in the stress of figuring out the next quarter's goals and disappear into their cave, only emerging once they have a high-fidelity plan to share. What's missing is input from your partners – they want to be part of the process of coming up with the plans, not just receive them as manna from heaven after you've tied them up with a bow. This is true even in companies that officially follow a more waterfall-like (yuck!) product development process, where UX takes completed product requirements and makes mocks that engineering then accepts and writes the code for. Leaving aside my distaste for waterfall product development, this process doesn't preclude involving engineering and design earlier on to test ideas and discuss possible priorities. I guarantee every hour spent brainstorming with your engineering and design partners about plans is some of the highest-ROI use of your time it's possible to find.

Lastly, find opportunities for your partners to present the team's plans or updates wherever possible. Often this falls to PMs by default, but I've seen great results when PMs generously share their toys with engineering and design, asking them to talk about the OKRs with management or give updates at a business review. It gives them a chance to be in the limelight, which increases their sense of being included and valued, and takes some pressure off you, too. Double win!

Action items

- ☐ Schedule a recurring 1:1 with your engineering lead and design counterpart

- ☐ Use GenAI to create a list of questions to discuss with your engineering and design counterparts about working styles

MEET KEY PARTNERS

▶ **Timing**

- Week 5

- Spend a couple of weeks forming initial relationships, then tend them periodically

▶ **Goal of chapter**

- Map out the key relationships with peripheral teams and functions you need and schedule time to meet them

▶ **Background: Why is this needed?**

- It takes a village to make a good product, and that village needs more than just PMs, engineers, and designers. At some point you'll also want input and advice from other functions and also other product teams outside your immediate area, and it helps to already have a relationship established so that the first thing they hear from you isn't "Hi, I need you to spend a couple of hours doing me a favor!"

▶ **Resources**

- Stakeholder Mapping 101: A Product Manager's Guide (QR1)

- Product Stakeholders: Categorize, Map, and Manage (QR2)

- 10 Tips for Building Strong Relationships with Stakeholders in Product Management (QR3)

- How Product Managers Should Deal with Different Stakeholder Types (QR4)

QR1   QR2   QR3

QR4

One mistake I've made in the past is spending all my time with my immediate team: engineers and designers. While this definitely pays off in terms of trust and getting to know the product inside and out, it led to hitting a wall quickly as soon as I needed to do something that went outside my sandbox – which didn't take long. Products tend to be complex and have a lot of interdependent parts: You're not an island, and neither is your team.

Which partners do you need?

There are two types of partners you'll want: 1) those who are necessary to achieve your goals, and 2) those whose goals overlap with your own. Hopefully there are plenty of people who are in *both* groups, but this is not guaranteed.

The first group contains functions like Legal, Compliance, Security, etc. They can block your efforts (for good reasons!), so it pays to have sympathetic ears there. Plus if you have a partner you can bring in early on your initiatives, you can surface issues long before you get close to launch day. Ideally your company would have a structured program for partnerships/engagement with these teams, but whether or not this is the case, try to find individuals from all of the relevant teams whom you can partner with – build the relationship, and keep them informed about what's happening.

The second group contains functions like Marketing, Business Development, other Product teams, etc. The people in these functions will have similar goals to yours. Say you want to grow the user base of your product. Marketing will definitely have an almost-identical goal. Business Development probably wants to sign more partners, and you can work with them to help them identify which partners will pay off the most in terms of growth. And there are probably other Product teams that will benefit from your product growing, and hence would be interested to at least share ideas, or even go as far as having a shared KPI or project goal.

Don't make the classic human error of rounding small weights to zero. You definitely want to work your way down the list of partners in order of influence and information, but you should try not to draw a line in the list and then stop. The ideal situation for a PM is to know everyone in the whole company. This is obviously not possible after a company reaches a certain size, but "know more people" should nonetheless always be your mantra.

Using peers

One oft-overlooked valuable set of relationships is your PM peers. It's easy to fall into a pattern of only seeking out other PMs when you need a new feature from their team, or to complain about a bug you've found. But other PMs are both a rich source of information and also the best support network you will have – no-one else understands your pain quite like other people experiencing the same thing!

As we discussed earlier, information flow is a core part of the PM job – don't forget that applies to your peers as well as to you! PMs are information conduits, and connecting to other central nodes in the network will vastly increase your odds of picking up the right knowledge early. "What's going on in your part of the world?" is the right question to include in your conversations.

Bounce specific situations off them. "I'm doing X but facing problem Y. What do you think?" can lead to some excellent insights, and at the very least verbalizing something often helps you get more clarity.

Make sure you use your projection (see *Create a projection of yourself*) in relationships with peers. They should have a very clear picture of who you are and which topics you are interested in. Many times I've had an email out of the blue from another PM saying "I remember you were thinking about {topic Z} and I just met Person A (in cc) who is working on that with their team – you two should talk!" When this happens, thank the person! You want them to have a happy memory of having helped you.

Aside from information and advice, having a good group of other PMs you meet with regularly is super helpful for psychological support. Find a handful of friendly PMs and make time regularly to hang out.

Action items

☐ Complete your lists of supporting functions and related teams + their key people

☐ Plan your schedule for when to meet those people

☐ Book your first three intro calls with people

☐ Research existing peer networks at your company

☐ Reach out to another PM and ask for a coffee chat with no agenda beyond meeting each other and comparing notes about your jobs

MAINTAIN RELATIONSHIPS

▶ **Timing**

- Week 9

- Requires ongoing attention and tweaking

▶ **Goal of chapter**

- Set up a cadence for checking in with key partners

▶ **Background: Why is this needed?**

- Your network of relationships is an incredibly valuable asset that will depreciate quickly if you don't continue investing. Taking the time to plan how you will do so without incurring a huge time cost is well worth while.

▶ **Resources**

- 7 Tactics to Maintain Positive Stakeholder Relationships (QR1)

- How the best CEOs build lasting stakeholder relationships (QR2)

QR1

QR2

After you've had an intro meeting with someone, following up is vital for setting the relationship up for ongoing strength. You are turning the interaction from a one-time meeting into an ongoing exchange of value and information. If you do this well, you will become one of the best-connected people in your organization, meaning that other people will start to seek you out – exactly the position you want to be in.

Some tips:

▶ Make a note of anything you have promised to do for them or they have promised to do for you, and put a reminder in your calendar to follow up in a few days.

▶ Send each person a message within 48 hours after your meeting, thanking them for their time and referring to something you found valuable from the meeting.

▶ Mention to people who referred you to them, to help make more visible the influence webs (see next section).

▶ Note down who is interested in which topics, and who is knowledgeable in which topics. If you find a connection that could be useful, make it! If you come across information that could be useful to someone, send it to them.

Terminology soapbox: I *hate* the term "bi-weekly" because it is ambiguous. I recommend the wonderful word "fortnightly," meaning every 2 weeks.

Then going forward, the most obvious tool for building relationships is recurring 1:1 meetings. You will probably default to a weekly or maybe fortnightly cadence. And this is great: You'll build relationships quickly, and you'll make sure that your information flow is strong. But soon you will hit a point where your calendar is all meetings, and a lot of them are these recurring 1:1s. You'll reach a stage where you are looking for reasons to cancel them, to free up time so that you can make a dent in that to-do list that is growing by the minute.

There are two strategies: drop the cadence, or stay in touch via other means.

Dropping the cadence is an underrated tactic. Monthly 1:1s are fine for many relationships, because the situation just doesn't change that frequently. Then you complement this with ad hoc meetings as needed to unblock a project.

So why not just have ad hoc meetings, if a relationship is mostly focused on specific projects? This can work, but it risks (a) running down your mutual social capital to inefficient levels, and (b) doesn't give you a backstop to catch anything you might have missed.

Be careful how you communicate that you want to reduce the cadence of meetings with someone. For people whose calendars aren't as full as yours, this can come across as a rejection and a sign that they are not important to you – you don't want this, so make it clear that this is a response to your overloaded calendar, not a signal that you don't care.

Using other means to stay in touch usually means written communication. Sending out an update email to stakeholders is a good way to efficiently manage outward communications. Finding out if other people have an equivalent ritual can potentially provide the inward information flow.

An equivalent can be to find out where they track tasks or projects and peep in occasionally. Checking their Jira board and clicking around a little can give you a lot of insight about what they're doing. And on the flip side, sharing your project tracking artifacts with partners (so long as you update the artifacts!) can give them a nice zero-touch window into your team's priorities and activities.

Action items

- [ ] Fill in the template of key relationships and how you will maintain them

- [ ] Send a thank you email or message to someone who has helped you this week

- [ ] Schedule a reminder to yourself for every quarter to update your relationship management system

MAP INFLUENCE AND INFORMATION WEBS IN THE ORGANIZATION

▶ **Timing**

- Week 10

- Periodically update

▶ **Goal of chapter**

- Figure out where the hidden flows of influence and information are so that you can tap into them when needed

▶ **Background: Why is this needed?**

- Companies tend to be hierarchical, but the hierarchy is far from the only way that influence and information flow. Knowing who talks to whom and whose opinion matters to whom will help you a lot as you try to embed yourself in the network.

▶ **Resources**

- How to Build a Power Map for Your Project **(QR1)**

- 7 Internal Politics Situations You'll Encounter as a Product Manager **(QR2)**

- Stakeholder Analysis using the Power Interest Grid **(QR3)**

- Stakeholder mapping guide **(QR4)**

QR1   QR2   QR3

QR4

Information webs

Information flows in companies via connections between people. Some information flows are easy to see: broadcast emails or all-hands from executives. Most, however, are subtle and hidden: hallway conversations, chat messages, 1:1 meetings. You want to get a sense of how information flows around your organization so that you can (a) get the information you need, and (b) make sure your message gets out to the people you want to hear it.

> You could also visualize information flow as more of a cascade, like a river or waterfall, but I prefer the network analogy.

How to map information flow:

▶ Key question: Who talks to whom?

▶ Take a look at peoples' calendars. Who do they have recurring meetings with, especially 1:1 meetings? Which people are regularly in the same meetings together?

▶ Ask people straight out when you first meet them: who are the most important people for your success? Where do you get information from, and who do you most often transmit information to?

▶ Encode this knowledge somewhere where the relationships can be visible! A word document won't cut it, and a spreadsheet is possible but will be painful. You want a relational database, essentially.

▶ See section *Manage information flow* for more on handling information.

Influence webs

When making decisions, everyone has certain people whose opinions carry particular weight. You want to have a clear sense of where influence flows in your organization, so that you can tap into it rather than be blind to it. For example, you might have a Director of Product who will always go along with whatever their Principal Engineer recommends. Or a VP who will first check to see what their Chief of Staff thinks before committing to anything. In both cases, if you want buy-in from the former parties, you know exactly whom you need to convince first.

Mapping influence webs follows a similar process to mapping information, but you are looking for where the decision-making power is and where the more subtle power is – for example, to shape what topics even come up for discussion, to change people's minds about an idea, or to muster support or opposition for something.

How to map influence:

▶ Ask people straight out: Who has the power to veto suggestions? Whose support would be helpful for getting a project approved?

▶ Watch closely in larger meetings. Who speaks first, who takes the seat at the head of the table, whose voice closes off a discussion? Who do people look to in moments of uncertainty?

▶ Again, encode this knowledge somewhere you can use it and update it! This will be enormously valuable, but only if it is at your fingertips and up-to-date.

Lucidchart or Miro are good tool choices for drawing your maps, but there are plenty of mind-mapping software options out there. Don't agonize too much about the software, just pick something that you like and run with it. You could even do it on a whiteboard or use Post-its if you enjoy a more analog approach! The important part (as with everything in this book!) is to get started on it.

Action items

☐ Draw up your best guess at your organization's information web – don't agonize over it, just spend half an hour drawing dots and lines and see what you learn

☐ Draw up your best guess at your organization's influence web

USE YOUR MANAGER EFFECTIVELY

► **Timing**

- Week 5

- Half a day to set up

► **Goal of chapter**

- Develop a plan for how to get the most out of the relationship with your manager: how to update them, when to escalate to them, and what questions you should be asking at 1:1s

► **Background: Why is this needed?**

- Your manager is, after you, the person most invested in your success, and is one of the most powerful resources you have at your disposal to make faster progress. But they are busy and you are probably not their only report, so it's necessary to have a strategy for making the most out of the relationship.

► **Resources**

- Managing Your Boss **(QR1)**

- 11 Things Every Employee Should Do to Manage Up Effectively **(QR2)**

- The fine art of managing up **(QR3)**

- A product manager's guide to managing up **(QR4)**

- How to Ask for Feedback That Will Actually Help You **(QR5)**

QR1

QR2

QR3

QR4

QR5

Your manager is one of the most important determinants of your success. To some extent the die is already cast as soon as you accept the position – your manager is either skilled or unskilled, engaged or disengaged, proactive or reactive, and there isn't much you can do to change that. But regardless of your manager's innate qualities, there are actions you should be taking to make the most of that relationship.

Proactively updating your boss on what you are doing is important because although you might feel they must see all of the good work you're doing, you only represent a fraction of their responsibilities and concerns, and the attention you will get is proportionate.

Use your boss as a sanity check for what you are learning, and a course correction for where you are spending your time – see *Seek feedback*.

If your manager resists initial daily check ins, that's a bad sign. Diagnosing a bad fit is out of the scope of this book, but I have a lot of thoughts, so feel free to reach out.

When you first start, you should be meeting with your manager daily, so that you can ask questions and discuss what you're learning, and then as you ramp up you can reduce the cadence until you end up with a weekly 1:1.

I'm pretty opinionated about this: I think weekly 1:1s are the right approach. If you aren't meeting 1:1 with your manager weekly, then something is going wrong. Either they have too many direct reports, which is bad for you, or they're not adding much value to you, also bad, or you aren't moving quickly enough to have topics to discuss every week, also bad.

Here are the sorts of questions you should be asking your manager at your 1:1s:

▶ Am I prioritizing the right projects?

▶ Here are some key decisions I've made recently (or am about to make) – do you agree with the approach?

▶ Do you have new information about leadership's expectations or priorities that I need to know?

▶ Am I performing up to the standard you expect or are there gaps?

There are lots of variations on the above, obviously, and this is not a laundry list – you don't want to repeat them every time. But over the course of, say, a month, you should be covering all of the topics on that list. You'll also discover other key recurring topics that make sense for your situation, so make sure you note those down too.

Learn to escalate intelligently. The obviously wrong approach is to go to your manager as soon as you hit any roadblock or difficulty – if they wanted to solve all of these things themselves, they wouldn't have hired you. But often I see PMs lurching to the other end of the spectrum, which is to try to solve everything themselves and only report actual results and successes back to their manager. Your manager is a tool to be used in the pursuit of getting the right things done.

When should you escalate something?

▶ When you have a conflict with another person or team, and your attempts to solve it 1:1 have failed.

▶ When a particular decision has consequences beyond your immediate sphere of responsibility. This is an important one – PMs wield significant power to make decisions that reverberate through the product, and if you sense that this decision might be one of those, you might want to socialize it and potentially hand it over to your manager to make. You should still come in with a firm opinion.

▶ When you are having trouble working with a key partner (e.g. tech lead or designer) or stakeholder. If this continues it tends to make your life as a PM miserable and impossible, so escalate early and partner with your manager to find a solution.

▶ If something has gone wrong beyond the standard level of bugs and outages that your team deals with. Ideally your company/org should have some guidelines for how severe a problem needs to be to justify certain levels of escalation – the worse something is, the higher up the food chain it should go. If you don't have this, consider writing one and circulating it as a "this is how we're going to act going forward, to avoid any surprises" – surprises are bad.

Your goal with your manager is to leave them feeling confident that (a) if they give you a task it will get done well, and (b) if there is something they should know about you will promptly bring it to them. If this is the case, they will feel very relaxed about you and happy to have you on the team, which is a good place to be.

Action items

☐ Create a weekly update email template that fits your style and your manager's preferences

☐ Make yourself an escalation flowchart and validate with your manager

MEET YOUR SKIP-LEVEL MANAGER

▶ **Timing**

- Introductory meeting in week 3, then schedule a second one in week 10 and again at least every quarter
- An hour to prepare an agenda and book the meeting, half an hour for the meeting, an hour to follow up

▶ **Goal of chapter**

- Get comfortable with the idea of meeting your skip-level manager, and think about topics you should discuss with them

▶ **Background: Why is this needed?**

- Your management chain should be one of the best tools in your kit for getting stuff unblocked when needed, and ensuring that you're working on the highest-value topics. This means your manager primarily, but also their manager and potentially further up the chain.

▶ **Resources**

- 4 skip-level meeting questions (and tips to fuel your next meeting!) (QR1)
- Skip-Level Meeting Guide for Employees (QR2)

QR1

QR2

Although the person most critical to your success is your direct manager, your entire leadership chain also plays a big role. They make decisions about whether your team gets (or keeps!) resources, carry the narrative about your big projects and initiatives in executive meetings, and decide things like promotions and raises. So you want to have a good relationship and know what their goals are so you can shape your plans accordingly.

Ideally your skip-level manager (that is, your boss's boss) will proactively set up a time to meet you in the first month or so, but if they don't you should take the initiative. This initial meeting doesn't need to have an agenda (this goes for all of your intro calls) – it's fine to just want to introduce yourself, learn about them, and listen to their thoughts about your product and where you could add value.

I toyed with trying to use the term "grandboss" but was talked out of it by wiser heads.

Don't be afraid of reaching out to your skip-level manager. In the past I used to be very reluctant to message or even email executives, let alone book a meeting, because I knew that they were very busy. It took one of them sitting me down and reminding me that their job was to help their teams get the right things done, and without information flowing to them, they can't do this effectively. You're doing your skip-level manager a favor by reaching out proactively, and if you're taking up too much of their time they won't be shy about canceling or moving meetings.

What other meetings should you organize with your skip-level manager?

▶ Ad hoc meetings to unblock execution when you have a conflict with another team that you've been unable to resolve or when you don't have enough support or resources to get something done

▶ Regular meetings (say quarterly or so) to check in about what they're hearing from the rest of the org, and to give them updates on progress with your top initiatives and what is next on the roadmap.

▶ Once or twice a year you should get their advice on your career development. This isn't as a substitute for your manager, but as an invaluable extra element, since they are likely to have a better feel for the overall career landscape at the company and probably in other companies too. Also, you'll need their support to get promoted, so getting them on-side or at least taking their pulse early is helpful.

Your core aims with your skip-level are twofold: keep yourself top of mind for the right topics (see *Create a projection of yourself*) and extract the useful information they have that will help you make better decisions and get things done better.

You should also email them judiciously. A rapid follow-up email whenever they have either asked you to do something or raised a question goes a long way to building trust. And sending them a regular update on key projects will keep them informed and ensure you and your team are never far from their mind. For updates, err on the side of short-and-sweet rather than exhaustive – they have limited time, so you are going for landing a couple of key messages rather than a huge info dump. I've found the sweet spot to be a couple of sentences on the team's most important one to three initiatives with links to longer documents (e.g. PRDs, problem statements, one-pagers) if they want to know more.

All of the above applies to your skip-skip-level too, just watered down significantly in terms of frequency. Ideally you would get some face time with your skip-skip-level at least once per year, and be providing updates quarterly or so. Once again, don't be afraid of reaching out – the worst that can happen is they politely decline your request for a meeting.

Action items

☐ Book a meeting with your skip-level and tell them a few points you would like to cover

☐ Set yourself a quarterly reminder to reach out to your skip-level

YOUR INTERNAL BRAND

Reputation matters. Your ability to get your job done as a PM depends on people knowing who you are: that's the only way you'll get their attention when you need it. It's also the only way that the information you need to do your job will find you. Thinking about the long term, it's your reputation that will determine whether you get promoted and rewarded or left to languish. This section is all about creating an effective internal brand, to help you build the reputation you want and deserve.

CREATE A PROJECTION OF YOURSELF

▶ **Timing**

- ○ Week 2–3

- ○ Do once, update periodically

▶ **Goal of chapter**

- ○ Get a clear sense of how you want to be perceived internally, and create some "branding guidelines" for how to talk about yourself and supporting activities

▶ **Background: Why is this needed?**

- ○ You want to make sure that the right information and opportunities find you, but you can't be everywhere at once. So you need to make the time you do spend with people leave a clear impression that they will remember going forward. Your "shadow" will cover a lot more ground than you can, so we need to make sure that it's the right shape!

▶ **Resources**

- ○ A New Approach to Building Your Personal Brand (QR1)

- ○ 10 Golden Rules Of Personal Branding (QR2)

- ○ Personal user manual template (QR3)

- ○ Networking for nerds (QR4)

QR1

QR2

QR3

QR4

You're going to meet A LOT of people as a PM, many of them for only a short amount of time. Try to maximize how memorable you are so that people reach out to you proactively about topics relevant to you. For this, one method is to create a cartoon cutout of yourself to live in people's heads. This means simplifying yourself down to a couple of key points.

Another term for this is "creating a projection of yourself." Your "projection" is the concept that gets activated when people think of you, so that when they're talking about you that's what they mention.

For example: "Daniel is that PM with the colorful shirts who is really good at helping new colleagues onboard quickly." Obviously there are millions of other attributes that make up the complex being known as Daniel Thomason, but that projection contains just the three that I want to plant in a professional context: I'm a PM, you can recognize me by my colorful shirts, and I am skilled in onboarding others.

Careful with this: once you seed a projection it may last longer than you would like. Heaven help me if I ever abandon my colorful shirts.

The ultimate goal, of course, is to have the inverse operation occur: When people are thinking about "who do I know who is good at or at least associated with X", your name pops up in their head because your projection includes X. So for me, when people start thinking about onboarding newcomers, I want my name to pop into their heads.

Creating a projection is as simple as mentioning these points when you introduce yourself to someone else, and then trying to allude to them at least once during the conversation. You could also go as far as including it in your email footer to really drive the point home, but while this almost certainly works well it can start to smell a bit desperate. Putting it as your LinkedIn summary is a good middle ground, though!

Action items

☐ Create a personal brand summary you can refer to when needed

☐ Put a concise version of your projection in key places: LinkedIn, your email footer, internal profiles, etc.

☐ Make a list of behaviors that will support your brand

CHOOSE WHAT TO BE KNOWN FOR

▶ **Timing**

○ Week 2–3

○ Do once, update periodically

▶ **Goal of chapter**

○ Develop a crisp sense of which tasks and projects you want to be involved in and which you want to avoid, so that you can position yourself accordingly

▶ **Background: Why is this needed?**

○ If you don't proactively position yourself, you will be positioned by others in a way that may not suit you – take the reins!

▶ **Resources**

○ *Reinventing You: Define Your Brand, Imagine Your Future* by Dorie Clark

○ How to Build Your Personal Brand at Work **(QR1)**

○ What do you want to be known for? **(QR2)**

QR1

QR2

Creating a projection of yourself works well for the long tail of loose ties, but your immediate circle will get to know you as more than just a single sentence summary. There is opportunity here as well as danger.

The opportunity is in being very conscious of how you want to spend your time and which skills you want to develop, and then making sure people know that you are the go-to person for those tasks.

Let's say you want to be known as the data-savvy PM. You start mentioning to your team that you love analyzing data, and whenever you get the chance you send out emails and messages with some tidbits you've turned up with the queries you've been running. Pretty soon it will become a self-fulfilling prophecy as people start to come to you when they have data questions or projects with a big analytical component.

But herein lies the danger, too: The self-fulfilling prophecy works even if you didn't want it to.

For example, you are a diligent, helpful team member, so you pick up the unpleasant but necessary task of helping everyone renew their access to the logs. You write a guide for how to do it, and troubleshoot for the team members who get stuck. Trouble is, now every time there is a logs access problem people start coming to you. You don't want to just brush them off, so you spend more and more time on this rather than the PM work you were hired to do.

This is known as the "curse of competence."

To politely extricate yourself if you fall into one of these traps, the best method is to take a "teach them to fish" approach. Write a how-to guide for the task you've found yourself stuck with, and when someone asks you for help with it tell them that unfortunately you're super busy right now but luckily you wrote a guide about how to do it; would they like you to send it to them? Inevitably they will be very glad to get such a guide – it's better than remaining stuck! If you do this enough times, people will stop bothering you, plus you'll get credit for creating a useful artifact – win/win! Ideally, of course, you avoid being saddled with low-value work early on: Practice the key skill of saying a polite "Sorry, I won't have time for that" and then sticking to your guns. If the request is coming from someone above you on the food chain, tell them what your current priorities are and ask them what you should deprioritize in favor of what they're asking you to do. (Apply this with caution if it's your boss: Sometimes you just want to take the hit and do the menial labor to keep the peace.)

To decide what you want to be known for, think about where you would ideally like to spend your time. From that list, find a couple of topics where you are more skilled than the average person. These are where you want to double down. It will take a bit of effort, but less than you think.

For example, one of the amazing designers I work with enjoys running brainstorming and design thinking workshops. She ran a couple of great ones for our team, and so naturally we sang her praises widely. Other teams heard about this and asked her to run some workshops for them, and it didn't take long before she had added "workshop facilitator" as a big part of her official job description. And she's super happy about that, because she chose the right area in which to build a reputation.

Action items

☐ Write a list of tasks and topics you want to be involved in

☐ Write a list of tasks and topics you want to avoid

BUILD CREDIBILITY

▶ **Timing**

○ Week 3 onwards

▶ **Goal of chapter**

○ Create a list of ways that you will start building up trust and credibility with those around you, as a resource to draw on later

▶ **Background: Why is this needed?**

○ You're an unknown quantity when you start – no-one is sure whether you're going to be brilliant or an idiot. Proving that you are indeed brilliant takes time, but in the short term it's sufficient to build a reputation for being capable. People want to answer the question "Do I think this person's ideas are going to be great?" but that's hard to answer. So instead they implicitly substitute the question "Do I think this person is competent?" You want the answer to be a well-evidenced "Yes!"

▶ **Resources**

○ *The Five Dysfunctions of a Team: A Leadership Fable* by Patrick Lencioni

○ Tobi Lütke: The Trust Battery **(QR1)**

QR1

Initially your team will view anything you say or do with a healthy dose of skepticism. Probably they won't verbalize this, unless they are unusually blunt, but it will be there. Your job early on is to gain some credibility so that when the time comes for you to say "Trust me, we should do it this way," the message will actually land.

So how do you do this? There are a few simple behaviors that fill the trust battery over time as you patiently repeat them day after day.

Be present: Turn up to the team meetings. You can ease off from this later (e.g. you may not always want/need to attend the standups), but initially just being constantly visible to the team will help a huge amount.

Ask questions, but not the same questions multiple times. People love helping, but they get annoyed with helping someone who doesn't want to learn. Bonus marks: When you learn something, document and share it with the team.

Emanate humility and curiosity. You'll need to make some decisions and take positions on issues, but your odds of being wrong are fairly high and you should act like it. Seek feedback and respond warmly when people provide it. To be honest, this tip will also serve you well throughout your career, not just when you're starting out!

And lastly, find a couple of quick wins to ship early on. These don't have to be features, either – alleviating some pain point the team has is a great way to build influence and get people onside. For example, the team might hate how inefficient the current sprint planning process is – you could help fix that. Or there is an unnecessary divide between engineering and design – you could help bridge that divide. More about this idea in *Find quick wins*.

Action items

☐ Get invited to the team meetings, if you're not already attending

☐ Start a "quick wins" document and pick one to get done right away

MANAGE EXPECTATIONS

▶ Timing

○ Week 8

○ One and done; should take a few hours to come up with a draft, then an hour to iterate with your manager, then a few hours in total to socialize with your key stakeholders

▶ Goal of chapter

○ Create clear expectations of what you are going to achieve in your first year, so that at key milestones you can demonstrate progress (and so that you know if you're going in the right direction).

▶ Background: Why is this needed?

○ In many PM roles, and *especially a new PM role*, the definition of success is far from clear, which is related to the problem that the role isn't sharply defined; see the next section. This is both an opportunity and a giant gopher hole if you're not careful.

▶ Resources

○ From Confusion to Clarity: Master the Skill of Managing Expectations at Work **(QR1)**

○ How to manage expectations at work (and why it's important) **(QR2)**

○ Managing Expectations in Your First Year of a New Career **(QR3)**

QR1   QR2   QR3

Unlike a football or baseball game, jobs don't come with a nice clear-cut definition of success. There is no end zone or home plate, the rules are pretty fuzzy, and the umpires are also players! This means you need to craft your own playing field and tell people which game you're playing and what it will look like if you are winning. That is, managing expectations is a key part of your job, especially when you are an entirely new commodity.

But on the plus side, the snacks are much cheaper.

The biggest danger here is that people typically abhor a vacuum just as much as nature does, including in terms of assessing others. If you can come up with logical, clear criteria that you ask people to grade you against, they will usually adopt them happily. But if you don't do this, everyone will implicitly apply their own criteria, and these will differ by person and function – meaning that you are all but guaranteed to have missed them somewhere.

You want to set expectations of what you'll be doing in two ways:

1. How you'll spend your time

2. What value you'll try to create

If you make sure that every important stakeholder has the same answer for both of the above, you're in good shape.

Rough guide to expectations you should be setting by time period:

▶ Your goal for the first quarter should be learning, with a small amount of value-add: Ship some small feature or help the team sort out some process problem.

▶ In the second quarter, your goal should be to ship something tangible but also come up with a roadmap.

▶ In the second half of your first year, you should be aiming to move the needle on whichever metric is most important to your team.

Often "which metric" doesn't have an obvious answer. Your broader organization will typically have some North Star goal (e.g. growth, or cost, or reliability), but using that as your team's target is a bad idea because *you don't have any direct levers to move it.* What you have are indirect levers – that's why your team is responsible for whatever it is. For example, you are part of the growth org which wants more users. Your team can't magic up more users (that's more marketing's problem), but you are responsible for the onboarding flow, so you **can** do things aimed at improving conversion, such that every marketing dollar translates to more users on average. And then going one step further: You can't fully guarantee anything you do will improve conversion, but you have a lot more control over whether you ship what you've committed to shipping.

Output vs outcome measures

The story you want to tell is: We're targeting this metric because it will have an impact on the metric that you (my boss and my boss's boss) care about. At least for now, please judge the team's success (and therefore my success as a PM) based on this metric.

The first person you should review this with is your manager. Bring them a draft, get their feedback, adjust, and then bring them a final version for sign-off. After that, spread to your immediate stakeholders – you can either share your expectations document itself, or just discuss it in a 1:1. Mentioning it to your skip-level (see *Meet your skip-level manager*) is also a good idea, to get their feedback and make sure they are aligned with your plan.

Action items

- [ ] Write a list of which projects you will be focusing on in the next 3 to 6 months, and a rough allocation of your time to each, then share this with your manager

- [ ] Decide on a North Star metric for your role and validate with your manager
    - [ ] Bonus: update your personal brand collateral (see *Create a projection of yourself*) to refer to this North Star metric

CARVE OUT A TERRITORY

▶ **Timing**

○ Week 5

○ 2–3 hours, revisit as needed when you inevitably get reorg'd

▶ **Goal of chapter**

○ Know and be able to clearly explain what you and your team do so that other people know when to involve you in decisions or share information with you

▶ **Background: Why is this needed?**

○ Part of establishing yourself in a new company or organization is carving out a corner of the sandbox to own, and letting people know it. "This bit is mine, and I'm going to make it great" is the rhetoric.

▶ **Resources**

○ Carving Out Your Space: A Guide for B2B PMs (QR1)

○ Lessons in Product Management – Becoming a T-Shaped Product Manager (QR2)

○ Solo Product Person in a $10M Company – How Do You Define a Role and Set Boundaries? (QR3)

QR1

QR2

QR3

Apart from what you *do* in your role, the other key factor to define – because it won't necessarily be clearly defined when you arrive! – is what you *own*. That is: What are you responsible for? Which part of the business, which systems, which problems – what is your *product*?

To do that, you need a definition that will be meaningful to non-specialists – everyone outside your immediate team. That is, your definition needs to be short and only use fairly common terms.

▶ "I'm the PM for X microservice and I handle phalanging except where the phalange is used by team Y, since they do that themselves" – bad, too technical, and you lost me after the "except."

> My copyeditor suggested that I should use "widget" rather than "phalange" but I think the Friends reference will land.

▶ "I handle everything to do with signing people up for our product – from the minute they enter the landing page up until we need to collect their payment details" – good, crisp, talks in terms that everyone will understand.

This leads to another useful aspect of territory carving: It can be helpful to also define what you are **not**. In the example above that was "up until we need to collect their payment details", meaning that PM doesn't do anything about payments.

The best way to do this is to draw a verbal minimap for people. Here's what you do, and on the boundaries here are the people responsible for the adjacent territories. Bonus points if you can quickly mention an example of how you collaborate with those people. The strength of this is that it builds up a rich picture in people's heads, making it more likely that they will remember you and correctly identify (and hopefully tell others about!) what you do.

Apart from clarity of introductions, the other reason to clearly define a territory for yourself is that *often this will not have been done for you in advance*. Usually your manager will have identified the brightest lines in the sand and scoped the role accordingly, but inevitably there is a lot of iceberg under the surface.

For example, I was the PM for the identity verification flow at a neobank, taking over after the initial sign-up flow and passing to the product onboarding team after me. But the company also had a regional expansion product tribe that was heavily focused on growing a particular market, resulting in a grey area between the teams. Would they build new market-specific features for identity verification, or was my team expected to? Neither answer is wrong, but also neither answer was the obvious default position – I needed to actively work to define the boundaries of my team's territory.

Action items

- [ ] Create an elevator pitch for you and your team and test it out on someone

- [ ] Draw a mini-map of your adjacent teams and product areas to see how they fit together

YOUR EDUCATION

If you spend any time on LinkedIn or have attended any form of rah-rah corporate training, you've probably run into the breathlessly excited explanation about how 1% improvement every week turns into a massive 67% improvement by the end of the year, thanks to the magic of compounding! If that were strictly true – that just by making tiny improvements you will get twice as good at your job every 16 months – then it should be trivially easy to become a millionaire by age 30.

Unfortunately, it's not that simple. The main reason this is the case is because there is not one homogeneous pot of skill that you draw on for your job and that hence permanently compounds. For most jobs – and certainly for a PM – it's more like you have a bunch of different skills and knowledge you are drawing on, and in any given week you can improve one of them. But because it's just one of the inputs to your success, the compounding isn't nearly as aggressive.

That said, learning quickly is still one of the most critical determinants of success as a PM. You come in knowing nothing and probably missing at least a couple of skills you'll need to be effective, and the quicker you can close the gap, the faster you'll be able to create value.

The aim is to get to a place where you truly are the second-best source for any particular bit of knowledge (after the actual specialist), and where you are the *only* person who can synthesize everything well enough to provide high-probability bets on where the team should spend its time.

In a nutshell, the best way to do this is to listen, ask questions, and only talk to plant seeds for future knowledge to find you. Then as you build your knowledge and skills, you can start to slowly increase the amount of time you spend expressing your own ideas and opinions vs absorbing other people's.

This section goes into specific strategies to help you manage this effectively.

CHOOSE WHERE TO SPEND YOUR TIME

▶ **Timing**

- ○ Week 4

- ○ Refresh at 3 and 6 months

▶ **Goal of chapter**

- ○ Set an intention for how you will allocate your time to be maximally successful in the long run, and keep track of how well you are sticking to this (and adjust as needed)

▶ **Background: Why is this needed?**

- ○ One key lesson that applies to every job but particularly to product management is that time is your main resource: how you spend it will determine what you get back.

▶ **Resources**

- ○ Mastering the Art of Time – Guide for a Product Manager (QR1)

- ○ How a Product Manager Allocates Time (QR2)

- ○ Time Management Tips For Product Managers: How to Prioritize Your Work (QR3)

- ○ How to Have a More Productive Year (QR4)

QR1

QR2

QR3

QR4

Time is currency. You should spend it on what you value, and make sure you're getting a good return for your investment. But just like money, the world is full of ways to waste your time, so being thoughtful and deliberate is key.

There is always a temptation to throw yourself into everything as a PM, particularly when you are just starting out. You're energetic, have good ideas, and excel in getting things done, so let's put all of that to work! Plus, you want to prove that you are valuable and not just dead weight... Trouble is, execution work is at least somewhat at odds with strategic thinking and building a strong understanding of the problem space. Not entirely – at some point there is no substitute for getting your hands dirty. The trouble comes when all you have is dirty hands, and no intellectual justification for why you've been plugging away at these exact things.

I worked with a great head of operations who started 6 months after I did. We were in semi-crisis mode at the time, so he got stuck right into one of the most visible problems in our space. He met with the right stakeholders, spent time at the coalface seeing exactly what was happening, talked to his leads, and generally approached the problem intelligently. The only trouble was, as he confessed to me a few months later, the problem was a complete red herring. There was certainly trouble there, but it was neither the most pressing issue to solve nor was it even the root cause of the malaise he had correctly spotted. His instinct to roll up his sleeves was both laudable and broadly the correct approach, but the big missing piece was spending a bit more time initially triaging where the true value was.

Early on, a good rule of thumb is to do a breadth-first search rather than depth-first. That is, scout the whole landscape before you start peering under rocks. Keep a running list of questions and try to find answers as you go – this will help to guide you.

The first thing you should do in a new job is get an answer from your boss about what you and your team are trying to achieve (see *Manage expectations*). Then you should start to explore two questions: What problems are keeping the team from achieving this, and who needs to be involved to solve these problems effectively? This means you're simultaneously learning about the problem space and the organization.

Come up for air regularly. Check in with your boss and trusted stakeholders about whether you are spending your time learning about the right things. Otherwise, you guessed it – you risk going down a rabbit hole.

Try to attend as many meetings as you can but only as an observer. Resist picking up any actual work for as long as possible, because for the most part it will slow your pace of learning. To be explicit: You should prioritize learning for the first quarter, and allocate your time based on how much you'll learn. You should call this out to your boss and make sure they are okay with it – if they're not and expect you to start showing real results within the first quarter, that's a red flag.

Action items

- [ ] Write down how you intend to spend your time each week: List your main activities and projects, and the percentage of time you want to allocate to them

- [ ] Look back at a past week and tag each block of time with what the project and type of activity was, then compare your actual allocation to your ideal allocation

- [ ] Adjust your calendar to help align these two better (see *Control your calendar*)

KEEP TRACK OF WHAT YOU DON'T KNOW

▶ **Timing**

- Start a document in Week 1, invest extra time in Week 3
- Update continually

▶ **Goal of chapter**

- Have a document and routine for recording new questions and finding answers to those questions

▶ **Background: Why is this needed?**

- You're optimizing for learning in your first 24 weeks, and asking then answering questions is the best way to do this. Writing this down will (a) force you to think more clearly about what you're asking, and (b) give you a record for future reference.

▶ **Resources**

- How To Identify Knowledge Gaps at Work (And What To Do About Them) (QR1)
- *Getting Things Done* by David Allen

QR1

If you're successful in meeting new people and finding good sources of knowledge, you will quickly reach the point where you unearth new questions far faster than you can answer them. This is a good thing! The key here is to keep track of those questions and have a process for finding answers.

Start a document with a running list of questions you have. Looking at your team's work in progress is the best way to kickstart this, because it tells you what the current priorities are, shines a light on where you are ignorant, and enhances your ability to add value quickly because you're looking into live topics.

You should constantly be asking questions. Take every opportunity to do this: 1:1 meetings are ideal, but also standups, all-hands, random hallway conversations – all good chances to find out something new. Don't overdo it, though: one or two questions per meeting quickly adds up to a lot of answers!

> Remember your ABC: Always Be... Curious? Collecting (questions)? Curating (enquiries)?

At the start, you probably want a daily touchpoint with your manager just for asking questions, and then it can ease back to a less regular cadence once your ratio of questions to answers starts to shift, and as your internal network grows. Ask your manager if you can set up a 15 to 30 minute daily sync for the first few weeks.

One way to augment this is to have a shared questions document with your manager, so that they can update it asynchronously. Caution: This shouldn't *replace* the in-person touchpoint, just make it more productive – you still want to have a guaranteed place to ask your questions, and an opportunity to turn those questions into more of a discussion when they immediately spark more thoughts. Asynchronous communication misses this spontaneous generation aspect. If you and your manager are both proactive about updating the document, you can probably get away with face-to-face meetings once or twice per week, so this can work well if your manager's calendar is overflowing.

Be a good citizen: If there's not already an onboarding document, use your list of questions as the seed for one. Even if there is, add to it as you learn things, so that the next person can onboard even faster. After all, you might be the one hiring and managing them!

Ask the stupid questions early

You genuinely have a free pass at "stupid" questions when you've just arrived in a team, because people know that what seems obvious to them will not be obvious to anyone who isn't constantly immersed in that world.

Pro tip: If you're really scared you're about to ask something stupid, preface it with "Could I ask a stupid question?" Invariably someone will say "There's no such thing as stupid questions!" and end up meaning it. The trick is, don't ask the same person the stupid question twice. Once you have the answer, document it somewhere. Bonus marks for documenting this in a way that can be used for onboarding the next person.

An exception to this is questions where you want to elicit different opinions, so you might ask them multiple times. "What happens if a user doesn't have a credit card?" is a stupid question that you should only ask once and then write down. "What are the team's top priorities for this year?" is a question that you could (and probably should!) ask different people.

The best stupid questions are the ones that end up identifying some illogical aspect of the product that no-one has bothered to question before. Your trouble is that you don't know which of the things that seem strange to you are in this category and which are Chesterton's fences. The only way to find out is to ask enough questions and use your brain.

Be quietly critical of the answers you receive, too. Always apply the "Does this actually make sense?" lens, and keep probing if something fails that test. This is how you find pockets of gold hidden in plain sight.

Action items

☐ Pick a place to record questions you have and start writing them down (by this stage you definitely have some – spend 5 minutes to mine you brain for them)

☐ Create an "open questions" document and share it with your manager

    ☐ Bonus: put a link to it in your 1:1 notes document

USE YOUR FRESH EYES: TEST THE PRODUCT AND COMPETITORS' PRODUCTS, AND DOCUMENT

▶ **Timing**

- Get access to the product right away

- Week 6 or so present your findings and thoughts

- Consider doing this again at the 6-month mark

▶ **Goal of chapter**

- Get access to your product and have a place to make structured observations

▶ **Background: Why is this needed?**

- Your product is the reason you exist, so you should be the expert in how it works. To get a truly good sense of what you should be prioritizing, you need to experience your product the way users experience it. This isn't a substitute for effective user research – see the next chapter – but is a vital and immediately accessible complement.

▶ **Resources**

- How to Do a Competitive Product Analysis **(QR1)**

- 8 User Tests to Help You Learn From Your Competitors **(QR2)**

- Product Manager's Power Move: Competitor Analysis **(QR3)**

- Competitive Product Analysis: The Full Guide 2024 **(QR4)**

- Competitor Analysis for Product Managers: Steps, Tools, and Templates **(QR5)**

QR1   QR2   QR3

QR4   QR5

One of the first things you should do when you take on a new PM role is to get access to the product. Download or sign up for the live, production version, but also work out how to set up a test environment too, so that you can safely mess around without either endangering your own data or messing up the metrics!

From the start, jot down notes about your impressions and questions. What feels good, what is confusing, what is annoying? Use these notes to seed your conversations with people early on, to find out why things are the way they are. Do the same for a couple of competitors' products, to compare and contrast.

Once you have a good sense of the main points you want to convey, take screenshots of your flow and one or two competitor flows, put them into a slide deck and annotate with your thoughts. Run this by someone in UX first to get their reactions, then present to the team.

Important: Preface your presentation with a suitably humble disclaimer about this just being your reflections, rather than a definitive judgment or rigorous research. It's easy to get people's backs up otherwise.

Just be aware: often these artifacts end up getting shared waaaaay up the chain, so invest a bit of time in polish.

At the end of your presentation, include three proposed actions to improve the situation. Ideally these should be more geared towards *figuring out* a certain thing rather than "We should do exactly this". For example, "Test whether customers will respond better to a CTA that emphasizes safety" rather than "Change the button to say 'Secure my data now'". The tone you want to convey is that you've found an opportunity for improvement and would like to explore it together with the team, not a list of tasks you are now handing over. Put some care into the presentation, because this is likely to be an artifact that gets widely shared – you want it to be understandable on its own, and also for people to be impressed with your work.

If this is well received, consider scheduling time to repeat the exercise in 6 months to see how much progress has been made on the points you raised, and to identify the next set of priority areas.

Action items

☐ Create a slide deck with structured observations about your product

☐ Create a slide deck with structured observations about your product

GET FACE-TO-FACE WITH YOUR CUSTOMERS ASAP

▶ **Timing**

- Week 5

- Ongoing

▶ **Goal of chapter**

- Figure out how to get close to your customers, and create a routine that supports doing so regularly

▶ **Background: Why is this needed?**

- A risk at a big company is over-indexing on meeting stakeholders and learning about priorities and problems solely from internal sources. If you focus on this, you'll find a wealth of information and no shortage of ideas, and you might find yourself forgetting that the outside world exists (see also *Build your industry knowledge and network*).

- The best solution to this is to get as close to your customers as possible, as early as possible.

▶ **Resources**

- 6 Tips for Product-Led Customer Centricity (QR1)

- A Product Manager's Field Guide to Talking to Customers (QR2)

QR1

QR2

Solipsism is one of the biggest problems for PMs, and is especially prevalent (and dangerous!) in big companies. You start to forget that the real world and actual customers exist, and start to see your product solely through the lens of internal narratives and prioritization of features on a spreadsheet. Your product is serving real, living humans, and the minute you forget that, you will start to build the wrong things.

Luckily there is a straightforward cure for this: Get out of your office and go see your product in the wild. As close to actual wild observation as possible, but every company should have some mechanisms to at least let you get part of the way there.

I say *should*; unfortunately this is not guaranteed. If your company doesn't have it, you'll have to roll your own.

For example, hopefully your company has some sort of mechanism where you can shadow customer support agents or even take some customer calls yourself – if so, sign up right away. Even if this doesn't exist, get access to recordings of actual customer calls and data on customer feedback.

Even better than support calls, though, is to see the product being used live and talk to actual customers in their native environment. If you're a B2B PM, see if your sales team will connect you with some customers you could visit and sit with, or if you are a B2C PM figure out how to observe real users in the wild. This means figuring out where your customers are when they use your product, and then going there. If you're the PM for a dating app, maybe people are browsing profiles in a coffee shop, so you could hang out in Starbucks and subtly peer at people's phones. Or if your product is a mobile game, people are probably playing it (or a competitor's product) on their commute, so hang out in trains and buses for a while.

These are very hit-and-miss methods for finding real users, of course. The highest accuracy method is to contact real users and ask if you can meet them and observe them using your product. Your User Research and/or Marketing teams should be able to help you here.

Important: Looking at the data and reading user research studies isn't enough! Nor is taking part in user research as an interviewer or note-taker – UX research is fantastic and super helpful, but not the same as actually watching people use your product in their normal setting.

One cheat code if you are a B2C PM: Get your friends and family to sign up for the product and use it while you sit quietly and take notes. Don't interfere or help, because you wouldn't normally be in the room while they used it, but do ask them to narrate aloud as much as they feel comfortable.

Use the observations you make while watching customers to seed your questions and ideas for features and improvements. Turn these observations into a lightweight presentation and show it to your team. It can be as simple as a few slides with screenshots of the product and questions/thoughts from watching the users, or as intense as a full blow-by-blow review – don't be intimidated by a sense of what this "should" be, though, since the important part is just getting the thoughts in front of the team at all.

Bonus: Once you've shown how valuable it is to observe customers like this, hopefully people from your team will want to join you in doing so! UX often needs zero persuasion here, but if you have engineers start to ask if they can come along on your ethnography excursions, then you know you've done a good job. And encourage this – there is nothing as motivated as an engineer who has had the visceral experience of watching a customer struggle with the product.

Action items

- ☐ Start a customer observations and insights document

- ☐ Send an email to Customer Service team asking to shadow them or do a shift

- ☐ Start a "Where are my customers?" document for understanding your marketing channels

FIND GOOD INFORMATION

▶ **Timing**

○ Week 7/8

○ Take a few weeks to do this well once, then consider refreshing periodically

▶ **Goal of chapter**

○ Create a list of different functions/people to talk to about your product and priorities, and take notes on the perspectives they share

▶ **Background: Why is this needed?**

○ Your job is to get an accurate picture of reality so that you can make the best decisions, and for that you need multiple viewpoints from accurate sources

▶ **Resources**

○ How To Build a Product Knowledge Base – Tips for Product Teams (QR1)

○ How Product Managers Manage Knowledge – Best Practices & Challenges (QR2)

○ The Product Manager's Guide to Utilizing Your Knowledge Base (QR3)

QR1

QR2

QR3

Information is your lifeblood as a PM so while talking to people will give you the most valuable information, this is far slower than reading documents and decks. Finding the right initial sources and then cascading from there will kickstart your learning.

Finding the right sources

Go wide before you go deep. This is both because (a) you need to contextualize what you're learning, and (b) you don't know yet what you can fully trust.

Age of and traffic to an artifact are both key indicators: fresher is generally better, but frequently used beats this. Also, extremely fresh can be dangerous, because that means non-battle-tested. You want something that has a comment history, preferably from at least a few senior people.

You should consider a wide range of sources: people, documents, recordings from all-hands, mocks/wireframes, external articles, emails, messages, whatever you can find.

Snowball from one source to the next: Most artifacts have links to other documents or decks – these will help build yet another layer of your understanding. Try to finish one artifact fully before you hit the links, unless the links provide critical context, otherwise you can end up in a Wikipedia rabbit hole situation.

See https:// xkcd. com/214/.

If you find something that looks interesting that you don't have time for or that is too peripheral to your current investigation, save it somewhere, ideally with a note to yourself about the context in which you found it – this can help a bunch when you get time to consume it. The "Read later" feature in Chrome is your friend here, although for this not to end up just as a graveyard for your hopes and best intentions, you need to schedule time to actually read what you put there (see *Make time for important but non-urgent work*).

Triangulating the truth

"Say not, 'I have found the truth,' but rather, 'I have found a truth.'" – Kahlil Gibran

Information from one source is probably best described as "anecdotal." If the source is robust (see above) then maybe you can treat it as trustworthy, but even then I would be cautious. You should only fully trust the evidence of your own eyes, and even then…

Here's the bad news: Information goes out of date, information is coloured invisibly by assumptions, information sometimes is created to support a particular agenda, information is incomplete. The good news: …er, I guess that's kind of why you have a job, at least in part?

How about information straight from multiple horses' mouths? Trouble is, people in regular contact tend to contaminate each other in terms of information, whereas you want the most uncorrelated sources you can find to get a genuine boost to accuracy.

You can combat this by looking widely around your company. Different functions typically offer hugely different views on the world. You'll obviously be talking to engineering, PMs in your area, and probably UX, but get out of this bubble early on to talk to marketing, customer support, operations, sales/BD, and finance (see *Meet key partners*).

Also talk to PMs from peripheral areas to yours. Now's not the best time to indiscriminately grow your network – you have too many people to meet at the moment to waste any slots in your calendar! – so you want to find someone outside your team/tribe/department but whose product touches or is related to yours in some way.

Action items

☐ Start a notes document to record your insights from conversations with different people

☐ Draw a mind map of the perspectives you uncover, linking the concepts that relate to one another, to start getting a sense of the *gestalt* of your space

FIGURE OUT HOW THINGS REALLY GET DONE IN YOUR ORG

▶ **Timing**

- Week 9

- Will take a few weeks

▶ **Goal of chapter**

- Figure out how to get things done and what to do when something important to you gets stuck

▶ **Background: Why is this needed?**

- Usually there are two ways to get something done in a company: the official way, which is slow and somewhat random, and the hidden way, which is quick and easy if you know how to use it.

- Your job as a PM is to know both.

▶ **Resources**

- Product Management Team Structure (QR1)

- Systems Thinking for Product Managers (QR2)

- Navigating Internal Politics in Product Management: A Guide (QR3)

QR1

QR2

QR3

Imagine you are trying to get into a popular nightclub. The normal way to do so is to wait in line with everyone else and hope the bouncer lets you in. But if you broaden your sights a little, there are plenty of other paths to achieving your objective of getting in: You could call a celebrity friend and get them to talk to the bouncer, you could sneak in through the back door, you could bribe someone to let them cut in front of you, etc. Not all of these methods are safe and some are perhaps ethically questionable, but thinking about them gives you back much more agency over whether you get into the club or not.

Same story with getting product work done. There is usually an official process for making things happen, but there are always plenty of hidden ways. The hidden ways usually involve people using their influence to go around explicit processes or give an initiative a helping hand in prioritization.

Health warning: this is one of those realpolitik PM tips that rubs some people the wrong way. It's not pretty but it works.

Don't think of this as being an anti-pattern; it's there to give flexibility to the system. If the only way to get things done were through the formal process, important initiatives would go just as slowly as everything else, which is a bad outcome for the company. The company wants to have at least a two-speed process, and informal pathways are a fairly easy way to achieve that.

Your task – and it is an important one if you truly want to help your team and product shine! – is to understand the ways in which you can get your projects and features moving. This means mapping out ways you can make that happen.

How to map out informal pathways

Start by asking people how things get on the roadmap. You'll get an answer outlining the formal process. *Then* ask whether anything gets on the roadmap other than through this process – this is the answer you're looking for. Also ask how you would get something prioritized by another team outside the normal planning cycle (because this inevitably happens, so every team will have some way to circumvent their planning).

Next, find the organization's biggest priorities and look for initiatives and projects related to these. Work out how these ended up on teams' roadmaps. Hopefully a lot of them are there because the core product team put them there, but I will bet good money that at least 20% of the items made it there through some other means.

The best place to look for the hidden way to get things done is in the cracks between teams. Usually individual teams have a fairly strong decision-making process for items that just affect them, but the fun starts when you have one team that needs work from another team to get something done. You seldom get the happy accident of the work being equally important to the second team, so this is where backroom negotiation tends to kick in.

What to look for

You're looking for the names of people who can override the system to get something either (a) on a roadmap, or (b) moved through blocking processes faster (e.g. design critiques or launch signoffs).

Once you know who these people are, start building relationships. Do this early – trying to meet them only when you need their help is far too late.

More explicitly, what you will be doing at some stage is trading social and political capital (see *Build social and political capital*) for getting something important to you prioritized higher. If you don't have any capital, you can't make this trade.

Action items

- [ ] Write a Plan B document for what to do when something you're working on gets stuck

PLAN YOUR PROFESSIONAL DEVELOPMENT

▶ **Timing**

○ Week 9

○ Take half a day to do this well, then book an hour with your manager to talk about it

▶ **Goal of chapter**

○ Create a plan for your professional development and share it with your manager

▶ **Background: Why is this needed?**

○ Without conscious direction and some forethought, your growth will tend towards random – you want to be deliberate about it so that you can easily identify the right opportunities when they arise, and so that you are constantly building toward an outcome you want.

▶ **Resources**

○ 9 Ways to Boss Up and Crush Your Professional Development Goals (QR1)

○ Your Product Manager Career Path in 6 Steps (QR2)

○ How to Plan and Grow Your Product Management Career (QR3)

○ Cassie Peretore's skill spiderweb (QR4)

QR1

QR2

QR3

QR4

It's become a common bit of wisdom in the PM community to "treat your career like a product," but that's because it's good advice!

Often (and this applies to a bunch of areas, not just professional development) the person with the clearest vision will win, not necessarily the best ideas or the optimal execution. So even if there is someone more talented or hard-working competing for the same ultimate goal, if you are the one with a crisper narrative of where you're going, you'll still likely succeed.

You and your manager should be a team in this endeavor, but you are the team captain. The incentives are aligned, since your success reflects well on them, but ultimately it's your responsibility – you have a much higher stake in your own success than they do. Plus your professional development goals may eventually lead away from your current role/company, and that's hard for your manager to fully help with.

An easy way to start: Ask yourself which job you want in 5 years, then go and look online at job ads. Which skills does it require, what sort of experience, what are the recurring keywords in the ads?

What should you be learning?

There are three main sources of development: learning the theory from books, courses and conferences; practicing hands-on with projects you take on; and osmosis from the people you interact with. My friend Ben Maliel referred to these as the three Es: education, experience and exposure. You should look for all three in your job.

▶ **Education:** Theory is important, and there are plenty of great resources out there (see list at the end of the book for a selection). But you don't want to stop here – that knowledge won't really serve you if all you do is drink it in without then trying to apply/test it. And it's tempting to do so, because this is by far the easiest and most accessible type of learning!

▶ **Experience:** Learning from projects is the most powerful but also hardest type of learning. And there is a tension here between taking on projects that you know you can knock out of the park, to demonstrate that you're valuable, and taking on stretch projects to grow but with the risk that you won't nail them. As with many things, you want a balance. A good rule of thumb is that in any given year, you should be able to point to at least one project that is a little outside your comfort zone.

▶ **Exposure:** Surrounding yourself with great people is an underrated way to learn. You are the average of the five people you spend the most time with, as they say, and this also holds true professionally – you will start to emulate the habits of those you regularly work with, plus you will naturally absorb their knowledge. The key here is to try to pick the right people, which is not always easy!

As to *which skills* you should be learning, the task isn't to compensate for your weak points. Your current skills got you to where you are today, so you can't be all that deficient! "Well-rounded" is a consolation prize adjective people use when they can't think of anything nicer to say about someone. You should be targeted in what you develop, based on what you are trying to achieve. Often it's more valuable to double down on an existing strength rather than burn time and effort trying to fill in a weakness.

Action items

☐ Make a professional development plan for the skills you want to learn in the next year, and share it with your manager

BUILD YOUR INDUSTRY KNOWLEDGE AND NETWORK

▶ **Timing**

○ Week 12

○ Start spending time every week or two on this

▶ **Goal of chapter**

○ List the ways you will stay in touch with what's happening in your industry, and schedule time to make sure you do so

▶ **Background: Why is this needed?**

○ You build products within a given milieu, the particular environment and the global conditions that your company finds itself in. Staying plugged into this is vital for success: There is nothing more tragic than an excellent product launched at the wrong time that hence flopped.

▶ **Resources**

○ How to Build a Career in a New Industry (QR1)

○ 10 Communities Product Managers Should Join Today (QR2)

○ Networking in product management: Lessons from product experts (QR3)

○ Learning a completely new industry domain? (QR4)

QR1

QR2

QR3

QR4

Products are built in an office (or maybe not even, in this age of remote work!) but good products are built with a keen awareness that it's out in the world that success happens. Out there is where your customers and users are, where your competitors are, and where things are happening that will either lift you up or dash you on the rocks. As an excellent product manager, you need to stay in touch with the world outside – most importantly with your users (see *Get face-to-face with your customers ASAP*) but also with the broader industry you are part of.

One of the big reasons to make sure you're closely in touch with what is happening within your industry is that it will situate potential product ideas within a wider canvas of where competitors and potential partners are moving. New features and products are seldom intrinsically worthwhile, they have to be good at that time, given what everyone else is doing and the state of the world.

You also want to learn from other companies' ideas and best practices; there are no awards for working something out from first principles when you could have got there faster by observing those around you!

The other big benefit of trying to stay in touch with the industry is that it forces you to get out of the building. Particularly in big companies, you can end up in a dangerously solipsistic state, where the world outside the office seems like a nice dream – customers and competitors alike start to feel like made-up concepts in the game you play every day. Keeping a finger on the industry pulse will pour cold water over this comforting but deadly illusion!

The easy way to do this: subscribe to industry publications – newsletters, magazines, etc. If you see an article you particularly like, consider writing to the author to tell them you liked it and ask them follow-up questions – this can often lead to a good dialogue and a new connection.

Write to me if you liked this book – I love hearing from other PMs!

The harder but more rewarding way is to try to actually *meet* other people in the industry. Attending conferences is a way to jump-start this process, but you can also just cold message people on LinkedIn to see if they would like to have coffee (in person or virtual) some time. A bit nerve-wracking, but very effective at quickly growing your network! Rest assured that other people also want to grow their industry connections, so this will seldom be a totally unwelcome advance, and even if it is, the worst that can happen is that they ignore your message – no loss.

As tempting as it is to stay within product management circles, try to branch out into other disciplines – the actual practitioners within your industry. For example, if you are in a travel company, talk to travel agents or hotel managers; if you work in gaming, try to meet streamers or eSports coaches, etc.

Action items

- ☐ Write a list of ways in which you will keep in touch with what's happening in the industry

- ☐ Block time on your calendar to read relevant articles and books (I like a monthly cadence for this)

SEEK FEEDBACK

▶ Timing

- Week 10, then again periodically
- 30–60 minutes with each person you collect feedback from

▶ Goal of chapter

- Write a template request to people for feedback, and schedule time with them

▶ Background: Why is this needed?

- It's important to regularly calibrate yourself against external measures, to make sure you're not wandering wildly off course, and part of this means collecting feedback from key people.

▶ Resources

- How Asking for Feedback Can Power Your Career Growth **(QR1)**
- Set clear goals and expectations **(QR2)**
- Performance appraisal (peer and self assessments) **(QR3)**

QR1

QR2

QR3

A rapid feedback loop is the best tool for improvement – this goes for your product, but also for yourself.

Obviously your manager is the most important person to seek feedback from, but you should also approach:

▶ Your skip-level

▶ Your engineering and design counterparts

▶ Other PMs on your team

▶ Other key stakeholders

The goal here is not just to check whether you are doing a good job, although that's also important. It's to check whether you are working on the right things, and whether you are at least aware of what your key colleagues are thinking – ideally you are also closely aligned to them, but if you are out of alignment you should at least be aware of this tension.

With your manager and your skip-level, one of your goals in seeking feedback is to internalize their mental models. This means getting a sense of what's important to them, how they make decisions, how they evaluate opportunities, which people they need to impress, how they craft a story, etc. The more you can do this, the more you will be able to pick the right projects (where right = likely to succeed within your company and also helpful for your own development goals) and present them in a way that will be well-received.

With your engineering and design counterparts, your goals are to make sure that you are working together well and that you are working towards the same priorities. That is: Are you running in the same direction, and are you helping each other rather than hindering each other?

Check in about team goals and current priorities to see what they think and at the very least acknowledge their feedback, even if you don't make any changes – the fact that you genuinely listened will vastly increase the odds they will be supportive even when you are out of the room (and that's the real test).

Don't confuse this with needing your counterparts to *like* you. That helps, but it's not the goal – being an effective team is the goal.

Also check in about communication patterns, workflows, and responsibility split. Do they feel supported? Do they think you should be doing more in some areas? Ask them about how they feel the team is working together too – this is a shared topic that you should both be passionate about.

With other PMs and key stakeholders, you want to stay in touch with what they are working on and their overall priorities, and get their thoughts on what you're doing – both to improve the quality of your output, and also to reduce the chances of nasty surprises.

Share your work at many points on the granularity scale: high-level goals and strategies, as well as concrete features you're shipping. Your peers and other stakeholders might not always have time or interest in everything you share, but it's fairly low cost and has a chance of paying off quite big.

For feedback about your performance, here are the three questions you should ask:

▶ How am I doing overall?

▶ How am I doing on {specific skills/behaviors X, Y, Z}? (E.g. communication, supporting the team, prioritization, etc.)

▶ Do you have any other feedback you'd like to give me?

It can be threatening for people to provide negative/constructive feedback, and if you feel like that might be the case, you could either provide an anonymised method, or ask someone else you trust to collect the feedback and give it to you with the names removed.

Action items

☐ Write a template for requesting feedback from stakeholders that you can reuse

☐ Create a list of people you will want to get feedback from

☐ Block time on your calendar every quarter to ask for feedback

FIND OR CREATE THE RIGHT FORUMS TO BUBBLE UP ISSUES

▶ **Timing**

○ Week 8 or so

○ Couple of hours to figure out which forums you need, then revisit as priorities change

▶ **Goal of chapter**

○ Figure out your go-to places to bring questions and problems you can't resolve on your own, for the most important priorities you have

▶ **Background: Why is this needed?**

○ One of the ways I've failed in the past has been thinking that the buck stops with me on every issue. This tendency came from a good place – a desire to be "action-oriented" and to not add to other people's workload. But the trouble is, I was only one person (still am) and often I didn't have sufficient context or the right leverage to solve a given problem.

○ Instead, I needed a place where I could bring problems that were beyond my ability to solve unilaterally to get the right people involved.

▶ **Resources**

○ Navigating Internal Politics in Product Management: A Guide **(QR1)**

○ Create Forcing Functions To Get More Done **(QR2)**

QR1

QR2

As a PM your job can semi-accurately be described as finding problems and solving them. Invariably, the first half of this description ends up overwhelming the second half. Not every problem you find is within your sphere of responsibility nor your sphere of influence. So you need a way to take those problems and deliver them to the right people, the ones who are responsible for and capable of solving them. This becomes A LOT easier if you have dedicated forums, rather than needing to go from zero every time.

Sometimes it's not even "problems" per se that you're bringing to these forums, but rather just questions or useful information that other people should be aware of.

The two most useful forums in my experience are (a) with the other PMs from your squad/tribe/pod/whatever you call it, and (b) with the other functional leads in your immediate area.

It doesn't take much to make these meetings successful, but if you don't have certain elements they will likely be a waste of time. In my experience, the vital elements are: someone leading the meeting, an agenda, and someone taking notes and recording action items. Attach the agenda to the recurring calendar item (Google Calendar does this for you) and encourage people to add to it in advance if possible. Also have as many standard agenda items as makes sense; don't make it a rigid structure for the sake of it but it helps to have a few normal rituals (e.g. review metrics, record upcoming out-of-office time).

The meeting with other functional leads shouldn't be about project status updates unless there is a specific problem with a project that needs extra support. Do the status updates elsewhere, keep this forum for solving problems. Similarly, the meeting shouldn't be about inviting everyone who might feel offended about being left out, it's about solving problems that come up, so keep it to the group necessary to do so. I've found it most productive to have PMs, Engineering leads, and Design leads involved permanently, with other functions added ad hoc if there are specific items relevant to them. You might want to add more if you have functions core to your product – for example, I had our Compliance person as a permanent member of this group back when I worked on identity verification.

These meetings may not exist when you first arrive. If this is the case, try to get them set up – work with your manager to get the PMs one going, and just put a meeting on the calendar with the other functional leads. Hopefully your manager can effectively run the former (although I've seen plenty of PM managers who sadly can't), but you will almost certainly have to run the latter meeting to calibrate expectations for what it will involve and also to demonstrate how valuable it will be – engineers in particular are often allergic to having more meetings, but I've never had a tech lead who hasn't ended up a complete convert to the importance of the recurring leads sync after seeing how powerful it is for solving problems.

Action items

- ☐ Write a list of problem types and where you would bring them to resolve

IMPACT

This is what you're here for: creating impact for the business, adding value, moving the needle, etc. I'm sure you're eager to get stuck into this!

I'll caution you going in, though: The siren song of rolling up your sleeves and getting straight to work is one I am trying to warn you against. Yes, there are no doubt endless problems that need solving, and yes, one great way to learn about your problem space is by getting stuck in. But the risk is that all your time will get sucked into execution, leaving you no time to keep working on strong foundations or think bigger-picture. Balance is key!

All that said, you're right to be champing at the bit. Demonstrating impact early and often is critical to your success. So let's get into it.

PICK UP A SHOVEL

▶ **Timing**

- Read the chapter right away to help mitigate the desire to immediately jump in

- But start contributing around week 5

▶ **Goal of chapter**

- Plot out when to start actually trying to contribute to team projects and get "real" work done, and socialize this so that expectations are aligned

▶ **Background: Why is this needed?**

- As a PM, you primarily create value via your team, so you will be understandably eager to get stuck in. These early days are critical, however, for setting expectations about what your role will be, what responsibilities you will take on, and what you expect from the team.

▶ **Resources**

- Focus on high-impact, low-effort tasks (upper-left quadrant) to build early momentum – save high-effort projects for later (QR1)

QR1

As a new PM, there is a delicate line to tread between spending so long navel-gazing that people start to question your value, and jumping into execution so quickly that you cause harm because of missing context. Plus the quicker you start executing on projects, the less time you will have to meet people and learn about how the company and your product works and where the gaps are. But then again, some learning is best done by doing! Like I said: It's a delicate line to tread.

This whole book is about navigating that balance and not starving the more strategic activities in favor of short-term execution wins, but the topic for this particular chapter is when you should *first* start executing on something.

Don't try to contribute in any team meetings for the first week, just attend and listen. You will already have your hands full absorbing information without trying to understand processes too. From the second week onwards, start to ask some questions, but try not to get sucked into more active participation (e.g. running the meeting or shaping the agenda) until after your first month is done.

> You might think that you or your company is the exception to this, because there is just so much to do. You're not the exception.

Which meetings to join first?

▶ Standups are good for being visible to your new team and getting a sense for personalities, but make clear to everyone that you will only join as an observer first, since your updates will be quite boring for a while due to the onboarding.

▶ The planning session is the highest-value meeting you can attend, because it tells you a bunch of interesting things: How does the team decide what to work on? How do they assess how much work they can take on? What is the motivation level of the team members? How well do the different functions interact and collaborate? Resist the temptation to participate or offer any thoughts, just listen for the first month – you don't know enough to add value at this point! This is a real temptation, because it's likely that other people in the team will actively solicit your input – politely dodge these questions.

One month is the sweet spot for focusing on onboarding activities without any distractions. In organizations where they are behind the eight ball on hiring PMs, you may feel pressure to jump in quicker than this, but push back as hard as you can (see *Managing expectations*). They were clearly managing to get work done before you arrived, they can continue like this for another month while you find your feet and gain enough context so that you can make smart decisions rather than just flailing around.

After that first month, you'll know where the biggest opportunities lie and you'll have a clear sense of how things are done in the company, so then you can safely pick a project to pick up without the risk of causing harm.

Action items

☐ Create a high-level timeline for when you plan to start getting involved in the responsibilities you will eventually own

FIND QUICK WINS

▶ **Timing**

- Week 5

- Every day or two for the second month while you ramp up

▶ **Goal of chapter**

- Identify ways in which you can create visible value to the team early on while you are still learning

▶ **Background: Why is this needed?**

- PMs don't have the luxury of a job with obvious contributions that people can observe and comment on – engineers can fix some small bugs early on, designers can make a couple of mockups based on existing screens, but PMs are on their own. It's important to provide some visible value as quickly as you can, though, to establish a good reputation.

▶ **Resources**

- Deliver a quick win within your first 90 days by solving a small but meaningful problem and measuring, sharing, and celebrating the result **(QR1)**

- What is the 5 Whys framework? **(QR2)**

- 5 Ways To Make an Impact in Your First 90 Days of a New Job **(QR3)**

- How to Streamline Processes and Increase Efficiency in a Growing Tech Company **(QR4)**

QR1

QR2

QR3

QR4

Building trust in any relationship requires action: Doing things that help the other person, and following through on your commitments. So while the first few months of a new PM job should be mainly geared towards learning, that doesn't preclude finding useful things to do. You're looking for quick wins that genuinely add value to the team while ideally complementing your learning process.

Think of this as starting to assemble a portfolio of artifacts and improvements with your name on them. Over time these will add up to a pretty big pile of value you've added, even though each addition to the pile will be small and quick initially.

Some examples of tasks that add visible value while also helping you learn:

▶ Make flowcharts of a process or user flow

▶ Document the logic behind something

▶ Take notes on meetings and share them

▶ Record the questions you have and answers you find somewhere publicly accessible

Another quick win is to record ideas about what the team could be working on, and then circulate these ideas early to gather feedback. You will inevitably start thinking from day 1 about what features you want to ship when you finally start to get your hands dirty. Talk about these with wiser heads (tech lead, engineering manager, design lead) to get their feedback, and be ready to introduce it to the team after your first month. Important reminder: Your first ideas are probably bad, so go in with the mindset of trying to work out what is wrong with them and iterating toward something intelligent as quickly as possible. The quick win here is the iteration loop of having an idea → discussing it → putting some details around it → showing it to a wider audience → recording feedback → filing away for future reference. The team will see that you are collaborative and interested in finding the right things to work on, and you will end up with a pretty good sense of where to start building your roadmap (and more importantly, which are the tempting-but-wrong directions!).

One underrated quick win you can get stuck into early is to find things that the team doesn't like doing or that don't seem to be adding value, and finding a way to get rid of them.

The biggest problem facing most product teams is a lack of focus – too many plates spinning. And the biggest problem for most mature *products* is a lack of focus – too many extraneous bells and whistles. A good solution for both is to constantly be on the lookout for things to cut: meetings, low-value projects, features that no-one uses, onboarding screens that just add friction, etc.

Chesterton's fence = something that looks useless but actually serves a non-obvious but critical purpose.

Your best time to do this is when you are new, because you'll see with fresh eyes and ask the questions that everyone else has forgotten to ask. But you are also at the most dangerous point, because you don't know which things are relics of a bygone age vs Chesterton's fences.

The happy middle ground is to ask lots of questions rather than phrasing your ideas as commands or even suggestions initially. In practice, this means that when you find something in the product to change, your first step shouldn't be to write a ticket or a one-pager, but to note it down on your 1:1 document with your manager and your tech lead, to ask why it's there.

Restating the theme of this chapter explicitly: The best quick wins are when you notice things, write them down, and then bring other people's attention to them. You'll learn, they'll see that you are curious but suitably humble about your own knowledge, and eventually you'll turn over the right rock to find something valuable to do.

Action items

☐ Write a list of ideas for where you can add value in bite-sized ways, to refer to each day and week for inspiration

☐ Create a proposal to remove something that is no longer worth having around

DOCUMENT SOMETHING MISUNDERSTOOD

▶ **Timing**

- ○ Week 9

- ○ Half a day to write, then half a day a little later to correct and polish

▶ **Goal of chapter**

- ○ Identify places where more documentation could be useful and learn how to build up such a document from a skeleton through to a finished piece

▶ **Background: Why is this needed?**

- ○ In your initial exploration of your new area, you will definitely have run across multiple times when someone has said to you a variation of "Ah, the only person who really gets that is Person X." When you go to Person X they give you a good, probably long, verbal explanation of how it works. This is a great opportunity to improve the state of the world by writing the explanation down.

▶ **Resources**

- ○ The importance of documentation (QR1)

- ○ 5 Important Types Of Documentation For Product Management (QR2)

- ○ The Business Benefits of Investing in Product Documentation (QR3)

- ○ Why Documentation Is Essential for Anyone Managing Products (QR4)

QR1

QR2

QR3

QR4

Documenting things that are poorly-documented is already useful, but the real gain (and what you should focus on as a PM) is documenting something that people think they understand at least a bit but don't really. As Mark Twain is supposed to have said, "It ain't what you don't know that gets you into trouble. It's what you know for sure that just ain't so."

There is no record of Twain having written this but he's a common misattribution.

These will usually be conceptual things rather than technical things; people tend to have a healthy respect for the mysticism of engineering artifacts. The problematic areas are usually at the level of "why does this exist" or "how is this connected to this other thing" or "what does this mean for customers."

An example: People were very confused about how users could add credit cards to their Google account, and this caused problems because then conversations would get bogged down in misunderstandings about exactly which integration we were talking about. So I went and talked to enough people to build a clear understanding, and then wrote a document explaining all of the APIs with a table comparing the most salient features.

Obviously the key thing is to write this and then publish it widely, otherwise it's not helpful. Don't be scared to send out a mass email – people will tend to be very grateful! The email should be short, basically just "Ever wondered about this? Here you go!"

The ideal workflow is to write a draft document based on your early understanding, share it with one or two experts for feedback and corrections, iterate, then quickly get to a final version. Assume that you'll be wrong initially, and expose your mistakes to those who can easily spot and fix them. Publishing your first version without validating it is a mistake, but so is spending too long with a private document – these things only add value once they are out in the world!

One of the big reasons to write these explainer docs is to save yourself time. You're giving yourself a permanent artifact to give people, rather than needing to explain the same concept all over again. And better yet, you're probably also saving your team and your manager time too, since they no doubt get the same questions. You'll hit situations like this again in the future; the third time you find yourself in the middle of an ad hoc explanation about something, add "write explainer document about X" to your to-do list (see also *Make time for important but non-urgent work* about quadrant 2 work).

Action items

- ☐ Create a list of poorly- or mis-understood topics in your area

- ☐ Write a template email for publishing knowledge about a topic that you can reuse whenever you want to share a new factual document

LEARN HOW (REALLY) TO LAUNCH THINGS

▶ **Timing**

- Week 7–8

- Will unfold over a couple of weeks, probably

▶ **Goal of chapter**

- Learn how the launch process works in a low-stress situation

▶ **Background: Why is this needed?**

- There is always an implicit or explicit process around how things get launched, and learning it will be a prerequisite for getting anything done.

▶ **Resources**

- What are shadow processes and why do they matter in business? (QR1)

- Internal Communication Best Practices for a Product Launch (QR2)

QR1   QR2

Product teams create impact primarily by launching new features. If you're not launching, you're unlikely to be creating much value. And the faster you can launch and iterate, the faster you can create value. That means that knowing how to get a launch done is a pretty key skill in your toolbox. Ideally you won't be responsible for making the whole thing happen every time, and in fact the less direct involvement required from you the better, but ultimately if a launch gets stuck you'd better know how to unstick it. This is one of those "not necessarily your responsibility but definitely your problem" things that characterize the PM role.

Again, PM realpolitik warning here.

The explicit launch process will probably be something like "Get these approvals, put the release notes in this document, make sure customer support knows about it." This won't be hard but it will be slow when it's unfamiliar, so best to build up experience on a low-stress, non-time-sensitive feature first. Volunteer to help get the launch checklist done for something already in flight that isn't a top priority.

Hopefully there is documentation around how this works (if not, see the previous section!), but even if there is, it is a lot easier if you have live people who can advise you. Partner with an engineer on your team, and ideally find a PM buddy who has done this plenty of times before in your org, who can help unblock you and explain anything that is unclear. Make your own personal cheatsheet for future reference.

Then there's the implicit launch process, which exists even if there is a well-defined explicit process. This is when you need to inform certain stakeholders and get their blessing, review the feature with legal/compliance/privacy/security/whoever well before you are going live to make sure they won't block it at the eleventh hour. And for high-profile features, you'll need to make sure that the CPO/CTO/CEO know about it and are on board so they don't suddenly veto.

Hopefully the implicit process is more about greasing the wheels rather than navigating internal politics, but there will definitely be an implicit process, and the sooner you get a handle on it the less sad you will end up. There's nothing as demoralizing as following the checklist to the letter only to still have your baby launch derailed.

Part of *your* launch process (even if it's not on the explicit checklist) should be the post-launch internal comms, where you tell everyone what you shipped, why you did it, and how great it is. The best approach for this is to create a template early on that you then reuse every time; it will save you time and rescue you from the tyranny of the blank page that prevents many PMs from doing effective post-launch comms. Don't fall into the cookie-cutter trap of sending the same email every time with the feature name swapped out – give yourself some room for creativity. But the core elements of a good launch email don't really change, so there is a lot you can easily reuse.

Action items

☐ Write your own private guide to how launches *really* get done (make it very honest and plan never to share it)

☐ Create a post-launch internal comms template you can reuse (or adapt one if your company already has one you like)

    ☐ Important: Don't just use the same template everyone else uses because it's tradition; ask yourself what the important information to convey is!

SHIP SOMETHING WITH A NAME

▶ **Timing**

  ○ Week 13

  ○ Half a day initially to think about branding, and then ongoing time to keep it going

▶ **Goal of chapter**

  ○ Identify a project that you can ship that the org/company will be interested in, and do some branding work to give it a concrete identity

▶ **Background: Why is this needed?**

  ○ To achieve a suitable degree of recognition for yourself – and your team! – it's important to have people talking about something you've done. And unfortunately, the best way to achieve that is by shipping something fairly big with an exciting name.

▶ **Resources**

  ○ Internal branding plan for a project (QR1)

QR1

In many cases the PM job involves getting the little things done: fixing the copy on the error screen, trying a dozen experiments to see what sticks, decreasing latency by half a second, etc. In my experience, the cumulative effect of all of these small, patient interventions almost always has a bigger impact than a single big launch. But it's hard to convey that importance to busy execs, so instead in their mind you'll be relegated to a vague "seems to be doing a good but not amazing job."

Fight this not by ignoring the small things but by also finding something big you can ship, and *giving it a cool name* (or alternatively, bundle the little things into a named package). I'm very serious about this! People will hear about and remember the name even if they don't know anything about the details of the project or the ultimate impact it had.

You can use a very descriptive name like "Project 90%" (if you are trying to increase conversion), or something exciting but opaque like "The Tungsten Initiative," or a hybrid where you come up with a cool acronym that means something relevant to the project like "Project HAPPY (Hitting Advanced Projections for Profit Yearly)" – all have pros and cons.

	Examples	Pros	Cons
Descriptive name	Project 90% Speed Year Safety First	Immediate clarity Reminds people of the goal Easy to remember	A little boring? Potentially too reductive Leads to assumptions about what's included that may be wrong
Opaque name	The Tungsten Initiative Dionysus Redux Project Prism	Intriguing Lends itself well to a whole project branding approach	Harder to create the correct association with what the project is actually about Easier to lose control of the narrative
Hybrid (backronym)	Project HAPPY (Hitting Advanced Projections for Profit Yearly) MOON (Making Our Own Network)	Gives a catchy version for quick hooks as well as a descriptive version Works well with project branding GenAI makes it very easy to find good backronyms these days!	Backronyms can feel a little bit forced/silly Invariably the expansion of the acronym is quite long, probably hard to remember

The important part is that you talk about the project as often as possible, and include that name in every planning document and update you give. Test how well you've done by periodically asking people "Have you heard of Project X?" and gauge their reaction. If they haven't heard of it or are vague, give the elevator pitch and offer to send them the summary deck.

Speaking of which: make sure you have those two things too – an elevator pitch, explaining in 30 seconds what the project is and why it's so cool, and a beautiful summary deck giving some more detail. One crisp structure for an elevator pitch that I like: here's the world of today, here's a bad thing about that world, here's what we're doing about it, here's what the happy future will be.

Polish that deck, keep it up to date, put your name on it, and make sure it's open for anyone to share and comment – you'll end up with free internal publicity if you do this intelligently, because people will start talking about your project in their own conversations.

Then once you've actually shipped the big project, celebrate publicly! Have a launch party with the team, and send out an email to as many people as possible talking about how well it went. Cite some metrics and quote some customers, and be lavish in your praise and thanks to everyone who helped get it done.

Launch emails are better than messages because they provide a more permanent artifact for team members to reference in performance conversations.

You will clearly see the positive effects of shipping something with a name at two times: 1) when you are negotiating for more resources for your team, you can remind people that you shipped Project X and it will put your ask in the context of something they know about, and 2) at performance review and promotion time you (and your team members!) will have something very clear to talk about that you don't need to spend too much time explaining.

Action items

☐ Write an internal branding plan for a project you are planning

☐ Create a pitch deck for the project

PRESENT TO YOUR ORG

▶ Timing

- Week 20 or so

- A couple of half-day sessions to prepare a killer presentation and iterate

▶ Goal of chapter

- Craft a clear message that you want to present to the company about why you and your team are valuable and what brilliant work you're doing

▶ Background: Why is this needed?

- Your job involves two distinct tasks: 1) convince the company that the problem area you are focused on is valuable to solve, and 2) solve users' problems in that space. Most PMs take 1) as given or as one-and-done, whereas in reality it needs to be refreshed periodically.

▶ Resources

- 25 Ways to Nail Your Workplace Presentation (QR1)

- 6 Tips for Presenting to Your Board or Senior Leadership Team (QR2)

QR1   QR2

"There is only one thing in life worse than being talked about, and that is not being talked about." – Oscar Wilde

If a product team ships an amazing feature but no-one within the company knows it happened, does it really make an impact?

Every company has some sort of resource allocation process where projects and teams are assessed according to some measure of their ROI, and if you haven't stayed vocal about the "R" part of that acronym then you might become the victim of a reorg. Not all reorgs are bad, but every reorg is disruptive and uncomfortable for those on the receiving end of it.

Part of staying vocal means presenting to your org about what you've shipped and the value that you've created. Both of these are necessary – the "what you shipped" part will stick in people's minds, but the "how much value" part is necessary to provide a clear tick in executives' mental checklist for "Does this team justify its existence?"

Sling praise around very liberally during this presentation – name individual people who contributed to projects, and hype the whole team as the real hero. This includes cross-functional contributors to the project; this is an ideal time to cheaply build political capital. You'll accrue plenty of kudos from doing the presentation and via the inherent visibility of the PM role, so there is no need to hype yourself here; now's the chance to share the love.

In fact, this is a good opportunity to get other people in the team to present who may not usually get this sort of chance. Engineers are the best candidates for this, but huge bonus marks if you bring in a cross-functional collaborator to present on a project they were heavily involved in. Doing this shows off a few things: a) your team is a good place for people to grow their skills, b) your team has a high degree of centrality in the company graph, and c) you're skilled at collaboration with other functions.

Keep the presentation punchy, but have plenty of collateral in the appendix for people who want to read further or for when questions arise.

This presentation is also your chance to market your team's big exciting future plans, so make sure you slip those in too.

Tell a story with your presentation – humans love stories, and remember them.

1. This is what the world was like
2. But there was this problem, that had these bad effects
3. So we did this thing to fix it
4. Now here's how much better the world is!
5. [Bonus: And here are the next things we're thinking about in this space…]

Action items

☐ Create a presentation about your team and what work you're doing, and book time to present it

FUTURE SUCCESS

You're off to a great start, but you don't want to hit a plateau after a few months. Ideally your career trajectory mirrors the curve you want to see for your product: up and to the right! This section discusses the bigger-picture items that will help set you up for years to come.

And it's a game of compound interest: The sooner you start, the more benefit you'll get from this work. But it's challenging to find time for this, with the constant demands on your time from the latest project or sudden fire alarm. Time to refer back to the work you did in the chapter *Make time for important but non-urgent work* and put those focus time blocks to good use!

BUILD SOCIAL AND POLITICAL CAPITAL

▶ Timing

- From week 13 onwards

- This is an evergreen pursuit

▶ Goal of chapter

- Understand the importance of consciously building social and political capital, and how you can do so

▶ Background: Why is this needed?

- The world runs on traded favors much more so than on constant cold ROI calculations. And people are busy, so they frequently take a mental shortcut: they don't evaluate the virtues of the exact request you're making, instead they evaluate how they feel about *you*. So having a good reputation and favors you can cash in when you need to are critical determinants of your success and your team's ability to get things done!

▶ Resources

- How to build more powerful alliances at work (QR1)

- 5 Ways to Build Social Capital in the Workplace (QR2)

- Social Capital in the Workplace: Everything You Need to Know (QR3)

- A Guide to Building Social Capital at Work (QR4)

- Four Tips to Gain Influence in Your Organization (QR5)

QR1

QR2

QR3

QR4

QR5

As I've said before, it takes a village to build a product. And like a real village, product-building villages run on goodwill and a web of mutual obligations. As a PM, you sit at the heart of one of these webs. In fact you should be actively building it!

This is because you are constantly going to be asking people to do things that are slightly outside their strict job responsibilities, or asking for a team to prioritize something that isn't completely aligned with their interests. If the people on the other side of these requests like and respect you, then your chances of success are quite high. If they don't know you from Eve or worse yet, if they actively dislike you, then you're probably already dead in the water.

Put another way, your impact and your team's impact depend on people and teams over which you have no direct control. All you have is influence, so you'd better make sure that you have enough influence to get things done!

Social capital is formed from trust and goodwill. That is, people think they can rely on you, and people want nice things to happen to you. You build these by being reliable (shocking, I know!) and by helping other people.

Reliable means primarily delivering on what you commit to doing. Simple, but often not easy. You might forget, get busy, or have second thoughts about the commitment. But being reliable means finding a way to avoid these predictable problems. Have a good system for recording your commitments (see *Set up a system for closing the loop*), schedule time on your calendar for larger tasks (see *Control your calendar*), and if you do have second thoughts about something, rather than simply letting it slip, tell the person to whom you made the commitment about your change of heart. People tend to be fine with a clear "I'm not going to do that," but they hate being ghosted.

And helping other people is easier than it sounds. It's not always about prioritizing the new feature that team X wants your help building, although that is one of the horse-trading methods of generating (large amounts of) goodwill. It can be as simple as meeting with someone who wants your thoughts or just attention for a while, even if this doesn't lead immediately to concrete action. Or being generous and widely encompassing in your praise when a project ships (see *Ship something with a name*) – this is especially valuable for cross-functional teams that often get overlooked when celebrating project success (think Legal, Compliance, Security). Bottom line: You want people to get a warm feeling when they think of you.

One of my mentors said the recipe for career success is to be easy to work with and easy to cheer for.

You should allocate your capital-building efforts with a barbell strategy: most of the time spent on your core constituents whose help and cooperation will be constantly needed, and a small but meaningful chunk of time spent building capital further afield. The reason for the second half of the strategy is that you never know when you might need help from an unexpected quarter. Internal networks at companies tend to be denser than you expect, so having lots of people out in the wild with a positive opinion of you starts to create a virtuous cycle after a while.

Action items

- [ ] Write a list of capital-building activities you can do

- [ ] Pick one to three items from the list and schedule time for them

- [ ] Write a list of people and teams with whom you most need capital, to apply these activities toward

FORM A VISION

▶ Timing

- Start taking notes early, but only really try to document a real vision from week 18 onwards

- Will take many half-day sessions to pin down something great

▶ Goal of chapter

- Know when and how to form a vision for the team

▶ Background: Why is this needed?

- Without a vision you'll still get good things done but every planning will be harder, what you do may not contribute to some grander goal, and you will be more vulnerable to organizational shuffles. The team with a clear, crisp, compelling vision tends to attract resources much more easily than a team with just a roadmap.

- But you won't be ready to create a vision until a few months in, because you neither know enough nor do you have enough credibility with the team to sell a vision.

▶ Resources

- How to Define a Compelling Product Vision (QR1)

- Product Vision: How to Create One for Success in 2025 (QR2)

- Top 6 Qualities of a Product Vision and How to Develop Them (QR3)

- What is a product vision? Definition, template, and examples (QR4)

QR1

QR2

QR3

QR4

Execution is everyone's job, although if it doesn't go well then it is particularly your problem. But *vision* tends to solely be the domain of the PM.

There will never be a block of time that comes ready-made with the label "form a vision" – you're always too busy – so start early and chip away regularly, otherwise you'll end up without a vision at all (see *Make time for important but non-urgent work*). And no vision is a problem, because it means you'll end up shipping a random collection of features that at best show positive results on an A/B test.

> I've lost count of how many times I've cross-referenced that chapter by now... feels like if people only take away one learning from this book, surely that should be it!

As the Cheshire Cat said, which path you take "depends a good deal on where you want to get to." Part of your job as a PM is to figure out where you want to go and articulate it well enough that people around you can start working on how to get there.

In your vision, you're trying to articulate the "why" – what's the point of what you're doing? Ideally it should be linked to the visions and missions of the broader groups your team is part of. You should clearly articulate how your team's success will help the company.

Start thinking and writing about this early, but privately – you need to develop an opinion quickly, but it will be subtly wrong for a long time. Part of your job is to eventually rally everyone around the vision and strategy, so prematurely coming out with something half-baked is dangerous. Visions should only change once in a blue moon and they are costly to socialize and evangelize, so you should be pretty sure you have something solid before you bring it to center stage.

Talk about this privately with key stakeholders to bounce ideas around. Your manager is the first person to socialize a vision with, once you have a fleshed-out draft, followed by your tech lead and design lead.

Once you have something that your manager, tech lead and design lead are all comfortable with, the next step is to go up the chain one step to get buy-in from execs. You might be tempted to do this in a large forum to finish off multiple birds with one stone, but this is unwise – if the executive is critical of your vision then it's sunk from then on, no matter how much you revise it. You've just had a leader tell you it's dead in front of a bunch of people, and they will all remember this. Visions are too delicate and too important to skip steps – you have to nemawashi this. Book time with the exec alone or potentially with your manager there as moral support.

> This is a Japanese word which means "wrapping the roots." My first Head of Product (hi Tom!) taught it to me. It's a fancy way of saying you need to align your stakeholders quietly before you get formal sign-off in a big forum.

Once the exec is on board, get their approval in some visible and easily verifiable way (an email or leaving their name and a date stamp in an "approvals" section of a document are both good ways to achieve this). This helps in the future if you get pushback from anyone – pointing them to exec signoff tends to quiet opposition pretty effectively.

Once you have a vision and it's received the blessing of the powers that be, keep repeating it ad nauseum. You will quickly feel like you've heard it far too often, but you're the only one who thinks that. Your team and stakeholders haven't been exposed to it even a tenth as much as you have, so you need to repeat yourself far more often than you expect. My old manager had a rule of thumb that it takes nine repetitions for someone to really hear something. You don't have to labor it too much in any individual repetition, just sprinkle a reminder about it into meetings and documents as often as you can – quantity is better than intensity.

Action items

- ☐ Schedule time to work on the vision for your product

CREATE A STRATEGY

▶ **Timing**

- Start taking notes early, but only really try to document a real strategy from week 20 onwards

- Will take many half-day sessions to pin down something great

- Should come after the vision, ideally

▶ **Goal of chapter**

- Know when and how to create a strategy

▶ **Background: Why is this needed?**

- A solid strategy is indispensable because it (a) makes your quarterly/annual planning *much* easier since you have a more narrow sandbox in which to prioritize, and (b) saves you from endless local optimizations, allowing you to pursue a path that hopefully leads to a more global optimum!

▶ **Resources**

- A step-by-step guide to creating a winning product strategy (**QR1**)

- Product Strategy: What it Is and How to Build One (**QR2**)

- Product Strategy Template (**QR3**)

- How to Create a Product Strategy That Drives Results (**QR4**)

- Business Model Canvas (**QR5**)

QR1

QR2

QR3

QR4

QR5

What is a strategy? A strategy is just a way to connect your near-term plans with your long-term vision (if you skipped the previous section on forming a vision, read that first!). It says "Eventually we want to be here (i.e. closer to the vision in a meaningful way), and the way we think we can get there is by doing/being/having X."

Strategies need to be opinionated and they need to make explicit tradeoffs. A strategy that says "We'll win by being the best!" is useless. At the very least it needs to be "We'll win by being the best at X rather than Y."

That said, strategy is **hard**, and it takes a lot of time to create one. If you're a more junior PM, don't try to do this alone – involve your manager and other functional leads. But as the PM, you will almost certainly need to drive this, since no other function really has this in their wheelhouse. In the best teams I've seen Engineering Managers help drive strategic conversations, but it's hard without the PM on board.

> You might have a Strategy team of some stripe, but they're more likely to be driving *business* strategy rather than *product* strategy.

One reason that forming strategies is so difficult is that they need to emerge from the bottom and top simultaneously. Vision is necessarily top-down, near-term planning should always be bottom-up, but strategy needs to bridge the two. That's why the PM is the best/only person to drive it: You're the only member of the team with such a strong presence in both the weeds of the product and how it is situated in the broader context of the company/industry. As with a vision, your strategy needs to align with the broader strategy for your org and company. At the very least, it can't conflict with any higher-level strategy it is part of, but it's best if it is clearly complementary to those strategies.

You should aim to have a strategy written down and signed off by key stakeholders by the end of your first year. You should have some ideas written down by the end of your first quarter, a working draft after 6 months, and be pretty close to a final product after 9 months. Then, as with the vision, you should get buy-in for your strategy from your management chain first before evangelizing it outwards.

You can be working on your vision and strategy simultaneously, but ideally the vision should lead the strategy. This is because the vision is telling you where you're going – what does good look like? Whereas the strategy is an opinion about how to get there, which is hard to do well if you don't know where you're going first! Don't wait to have a fully buttoned-up vision before starting your strategy work, though: These things are best when they co-evolve.

Action items

- ☐ Schedule time to work on a strategy document

- ☐ Ask other PMs for their strategy docs to start learning what already exists

DEVIATE FROM AN EXISTING VISION AND STRATEGY

▶ **Timing**

- Simultaneously with developing your own vision and strategy (see previous chapters)

▶ **Goal of chapter**

- Figure out how to navigate an existing vision and strategy for the product that you now own and make these truly yours

▶ **Background: Why is this needed?**

- Product managers need to feel like they own the direction of the product, otherwise it's hard to feel truly invested. This comes from being a core part of setting the vision and strategy. If you've inherited a dominant vision and strategy, that's a challenge you'll need to navigate, particularly if you don't fully agree with it (which is all but certain).

▶ **Resources**

- How to Manage Stakeholders When Changing Product Strategy (QR1)

- Product Strategy Pivot: Communicating with Stakeholders (QR2)

- How to Successfully Pivot a Product (QR3)

QR1

QR2

QR3

For starters, it's a luxury to inherit a clear vision and strategy, so try to be grateful. Most of the time when you're hired for a PM position it's because there is nothing in place, just a gaping void that needs shaping into something clearer and more purposeful.

That said, you will probably disagree with some details of the existing vision and strategy, if not the whole thing. You were hired to be opinionated (your opinions should be strong but weakly held), and the vision and strategy are so fundamental to what you're doing that they are likely points of contention.

> "Strong opinions, weakly held" came from a Stanford professor named Paul Staffo. It's become a bit of a mantra in the startup world.

Step one is to gauge how aligned the team and stakeholders are to the existing vision and strategy. If they have fallen into a neglected, forgotten state, then you can fairly safely create new ones and start again, although for continuity you should at least reference the previous ones – call yours the "updated" strategy or 2.0 or something like that, to make clear that it's new but that you know the old one exists.

But if the vision and strategy are actively referenced and used to shape decisions, you will need to work with them. It will be easier to evolve them rather than try to wipe the slate clean. That is, you will genuinely need to make yours the 2.0 version rather than that being a polite fiction.

Either way, pick a legible planning period milestone (annual planning is a good one) and schedule a vision and strategy refresh workshop. Getting representation from all of the people who were strongly bought-in to the previous documents will be important for avoiding pushback and giving your new versions legitimacy. Also their input will hopefully be valuable!

Before you've done your refresh, try not to run against the existing vision and strategy too blatantly. You'll cause confusion and misalignment.

Even if you've inherited a stinker of a strategy, work out what you think you should be doing instead, and then see if you can shoehorn some of those ideas into the existing strategy. That way you can start to run in the correct direction but won't have to fight all your battles at once. Calling the features/approach that you're trying an experiment and emphasizing that the goal is to learn where to go next will tend to quiet calls that you're running counter to the strategy – it's very hard to be opposed to learning! And when you're ready to have the conversation about a new strategy, you can already point to the projects that fit it as evidence for your proposal.

Action items

- ☐ Write a list of the key stakeholders you will need to convince about any strategy pivot

CRAFT A ROADMAP

▶ Timing

- ○ Midway through your second planning quarter
- ○ Will realistically take several weeks of iteration

▶ Goal of chapter

- ○ Know when to write a roadmap and how to approach that in a new team

▶ Background: Why is this needed?

- ○ If there isn't a roadmap in place when you inherit the team – and it's a 50/50 chance there won't be, since you've been hired to fill a gap – then there is a strong temptation to throw yourself into this. Try to resist: It will consume a lot of time and you won't do it well because you don't know enough yet. Plus it is not the best way to learn.

▶ Resources

- ○ How to Build a Product Roadmap in 6½ Simple Steps (QR1)
- ○ Product Roadmap Templates (QR2)
- ○ How to Create a Product Roadmap: A Step-by-Step Guide (QR3)
- ○ Product Roadmap Templates & Examples (QR4)

QR1

QR2

QR3

QR4

A roadmap is one of those things that stakeholders will ask you for periodically. The trick is, the term means a few different things: guidance about the features you're planning, release dates for upcoming launches, or possibly something more akin to a strategic direction. In my opinion, a roadmap should only be doing the first of these – showing features you're building, planning to build next, or dreaming of building at some point. It shouldn't be used for concrete dates, since overly precise estimates are a good way to kill the usefulness. If people want dates then provide something more like a project tracker. And while a roadmap is not the same as the strategy, ideally the items on the roadmap are clearly linked back to the strategy.

I like the "now, next, later" form of roadmap, but regardless of which format you use, the goal is to give stakeholders a sense of what your team is actively working on now, what you're planning to do after that, and which features you think will be useful but aren't the current priority. This then acts as a critical tool for conversations with leads and execs about whether your priorities are right, with cross-functional teams about the support you need, and with your own team to illustrate where you're hoping to be in the coming months and years.

The right time for you to take over your team's roadmap is in your second quarter, after you have the lay of the land and know who's who. From all of your conversations and research you should have a pretty good idea of where to look for value, and you'll hopefully have kept your schedule clear enough that you can spend time setting up a process for evaluating opportunities, if one doesn't already exist.

Don't get too ambitious or look too far forward at this point. A year is the furthest out you should try to forecast initially. But mainly you are aiming to create a roadmap for whatever period your company uses as the standard planning period (likely quarter or half).

Enlist your boss and team partners to create the roadmap, don't try to do it alone. Do these meetings separately, starting with your boss: Tell them your ideas and how you're thinking about priorities, get their thoughts, and brainstorm possible areas of value together.

Before you can make a roadmap you need to know what you and your team are trying to achieve, and then make that very clear to everyone around you (see *Manage expectations*). Ideally you end up with one clear metric you are optimizing for each planning period, because then the calculation of the expected value of a given project becomes easy. If you can't boil it down to a single metric, explicitly record your conversion rate between all of the metrics you're left with, otherwise you are setting yourself up for protracted conversations or being overruled by those above you on the food chain.

For example, let's say your main goal is to increase conversion. You'll prioritize your feature ideas based on ROI where the "impact" is measured in expected uplift in conversion. Easy. But what if you want to increase conversion *and* decrease customer support costs? Both good goals, but different stakeholders will certainly differ in how important they think each is, even if they are not willing to come out and say this out loud. It's therefore best that you explicitly specify a conversion function – for example, a 1% increase in conversion is worth a 3% decrease in support costs. You'll likely need to defend this conversion, so make sure you have some convincing argument for how you came up with the numbers. But once people have accepted it then the prioritization conversation again collapses to a fairly easy one of tweaking the ROI numbers based on feedback.

As far as the roadmap goes, *how* you develop it is almost as important as the end result. People around you need to look at your process and think "Yes, that makes sense." If they can say that, even if they don't like the end result they will still probably let it happen; it's when people think you've made stupid decisions that you tend to get pushback. Make sure that you specify and explain how you ended up with the roadmap: Which methodology did you use to rank the items, and how did you ultimately decide what was in or out? People understand that business (heck, and life generally!) is about making tough decisions. They just want to see how the tough decisions got made and run it through their mental filter for whether it seems considered (rather than capricious or foolish).

Action items

- ☐ Schedule time to draw out your first roadmap

- ☐ Ask other PMs for their roadmaps, to see how it's typically done at your company

SELL YOUR ROADMAP TO STAKEHOLDERS

▶ **Timing**

- Simultaneous with roadmap

▶ **Goal of chapter**

- Identify how to keep stakeholders involved in creating your roadmap and ultimately get their buy-in and sign-off

▶ **Background: Why is this needed?**

- A roadmap with no buy-in is just fanfiction about your product. Even if you work at a company where product management has the power to set the agenda, it takes a village to bring a product to life, so you need other people to be truly on board. There are always other things they could do with their time if they don't really believe in your plan.

▶ **Resources**

- 8 Strategies for Selling a Roadmap to a Skeptic (QR1)

- 5 Tips to Get Stakeholders to Like – even Love – your Product Roadmap (QR2)

- Tips for Presenting Product Roadmaps: A Comprehensive Guide (QR3)

- How to Share Your Product Roadmap with Different Stakeholders (QR4)

- Roadmap Storytelling: How to Share Your Roadmap with Different Audiences (QR5)

QR1   QR2   QR3

QR4   QR5

A roadmap is never done. It is permanently under construction, and forever in the process of being socialized. Make your peace with this, and get to work. A simple test for how well you're doing is to ask three of your key stakeholders what is on your roadmap. If they give you something resembling your top priorities, albeit probably filtered through a lens of what is most interesting/important to them, all is well. If they give you a blank stare or say something way off base, you're in trouble. Go get that roadmap out in front of people.

There are really just two principles that help sell a roadmap: 1) people want to feel heard, and 2) people generally don't like surprises. So long as you've listened to people and given them an indication of what the final version of the roadmap (or strategy) is going to be, they'll tend to be supportive.

What about the exceptions to this – those who are still annoyed that you didn't pick up their pet project? This is where having a clear prioritization methodology is your best defence (see *Craft a roadmap*). If you choose roadmap items based on clear decision criteria, then it changes the conversation from "Why didn't you prioritize my project?" to "I disagree with the calculation you've used for prioritization." The latter is both much calmer and also easier to handle, since you will have much more expertise in your prioritization methodology than anyone else.

It's a lot of time investment to drive good buy-in, but it only takes one round of dealing with angry stakeholders to convince you of how important it is. Here's my 6-step process for roadmap buy-in:

1. Meet with key stakeholders before you start drafting the roadmap, to get their input. Don't make the mistake of asking "What should we do next quarter?" because then you'll be in an awkward position when their ideas are bad. Instead, ask "We're starting to think about next quarter, anything top of mind for you we should be aware of?"

2. Put out a wide invitation for people to submit ideas and requests, through some impersonal process (e.g. a Google Form). This is the chance for people to make specific asks, but because it's arms-length it will be much easier to say no. Better yet, if an idea is fundamentally good but not your top priority, don't say no, say "not yet" and put it into a backlog that you will genuinely revisit at some point. Important: Make

sure you respond to all submissions! Nothing annoys/disappoints people more than a sense that they are just screaming into the void.

3. Meet with key stakeholders again after you have a mostly-complete draft, to get their initial reactions and feedback. A neutral reaction is fine, the only red flag is an abrupt look of horror or outrage. You're mainly ensuring they are not going to send an angry email to your boss asking why feature X isn't on the roadmap.

4. Meet with your boss and your team partners (tech lead, design lead) when you have a final draft. Start by asking for high-level feedback – is the general direction right, and are you pursuing the right goals. Then get into the details and hone the specifics. This will be time-intensive but critical: Once you're through this step, you're almost home.

5. Present the roadmap to your team and answer their questions. Bonus marks if you enlist your tech and design leads to present some/all of the roadmap, to convey an extra sense of ownership for those functions. Two good narratives to get them enthusiastic about this: showing off how central their function is to decision-making, and the career benefits to them personally from presenting to leadership.

6. Lastly, hold a big-tent meeting to present to anyone interested and answer their questions. Don't just read the roadmap, prepare a presentation to tell the story behind the roadmap. Ideally record this so that people who couldn't attend can still watch. Bonus: Use this presentation to remind people of your vision and strategy, and connect this to the roadmap.

Action items

☐ Make a list of the top threee to five stakeholders who need to be okay with your roadmap (you should have a pretty good idea of this from *Map influence and information webs in the organization*)

☐ Send your roadmap to each of them and offer to schedule time to discuss it in person if they want

CREATE A "NO" LIST

▶ **Timing**

- After strategy, before roadmap

- A few hours over a couple of iterations

▶ **Goal of chapter**

- Figure out what the likely siren songs are that will distract your team from the most important work, explicitly call out that you're not going to touch them yet, and get buy-in for that decision.

▶ **Background: Why is this needed?**

- If your roadmap only ever accretes items, you've got a problem. It's very likely you'll try to do a lot of them simultaneously, and without a clear criterion for selecting what makes sense given your broader goals, you might spin your wheels without getting anywhere.

▶ **Resources**

- Create a "NO List" (QR1)

- Why You Need A Not-To-Do List (QR2)

- A product manager's guide to saying no (QR3)

QR1

QR2

QR3

As a reminder: Your most precious resource as a PM is your time, and your team's time. A core part of your job is ensuring that you and your team are spending that time on the most effective uses possible. The main way to accomplish this is to craft a strong roadmap (see *Craft a roadmap*), but another helpful resource to maintain is a list of what you are *not* doing. This "no" list is a valuable defense against "magpie syndrome" where leads or execs can get so excited about a hot new trend or idea that they want to chase that they drag you and your team away from executing on your existing strategy.

This means the critical prerequisite to a "no" list is an effective strategy, because part of that strategy will be defining what you aren't going to chase right now. Plus it's hard to say "We're not doing these things" if you can't then immediately follow up with "...so that we can do *this thing* more effectively."

I have used the line "because it would be dumb to do those things" but do not recommend it.

Even with a clear strategy, though, maintaining an explicit list of what you're not going to run after at the moment is still helpful, because it is a tool that you, the team, and your stakeholders can use to maintain focus.

This list shouldn't just be items that came out of your prioritization methodology with a low ROI – that's what the prioritization exercise is for. Features or work that are a good idea and fit with the strategy but aren't the top priority right now should go in a backlog and then be revisited in future planning periods. In contrast, your "no" list is for items that are tempting to pursue due to potentially high ROI or loud support from elsewhere in the company, but that would dilute your focus and run counter to (or at least not be directly in line with) your strategy.

Try to have a fairly generic "no" list before people start to send you requests, so that you can point to the list as a reason for turning them down. Adding something to the list in response to a request is legitimate but disheartening for the requestor. That is, you want to say no to "internal tooling for operations teams" rather than rejecting "building dashboard X for team Y," because the former reads like a strategic decision while the latter feels like a personal slap in the face to team Y.

A "no" list is also a good tool for you personally. You should have a sense of where your time is best spent in terms of helping the team achieve its goals and growing your skills. Often there will be shiny distractions that demand your time, but that are way outside this optimal area. PMs are particularly vulnerable to this: Since you're involved in so many activities, you have a huge surface area for new projects and tasks to find you. Having a clear "no" list for yourself will help you resist these siren songs. You probably want to keep this list private – it comes across as a bit entitled – but share it with your manager to get their feedback and also enlist them to help you stick to it.

Action items

- [ ] Draft an email to stakeholders introducing your team's "no" list, and talk to your manager about it at your next 1:1 before sending it

- [ ] Write your own personal "no" list

CONCLUSION

So that's it: By now, you should be well on your way to success in your new PM job. We've covered a lot of ground. You should have a set of productive habits and routines, a strong network of relationships, a clear internal brand, a plan for your ongoing education, some early wins to point to, and a path to ever-increasing accomplishments over time.

That wasn't so hard, was it?

But seriously: Well done for making it this far. Product management is one of the most challenging but also rewarding roles in a tech company, but like many disciplines it's only really fun if you do it well. Taking the time to invest in strong foundations by reading this book will help make your work life as fulfilling and productive as possible.

Now I'll leave you with a call to action: Pay it forward! If you found any of the tips or action items in this book to be particularly helpful, go and share them with a colleague. Feel free to share the resources and worksheets, or even lend them your copy of the book if you think they'll like it.

And if you have questions I didn't cover or just want to say hi, please reach out. You can find my current contact information at dthomason.com – I love hearing from other PMs, particularly those who have read my book!

Best of luck in your product management career. Imagine me cheering for you from the sidelines in all of your professional endeavors.

– Daniel

SELECT BIBLIOGRAPHY

This is a non-exhaustive list of books that have been helpful to me in my career as a product manager.

Inspired: How To Create Products Customers Love, by Marty Cagan

The Hard Thing About Hard Things, by Ben Horowitz

High-Output Management, by Andy Grove

The Effective Executive, by Peter Drucker

The Five Dysfunctions of a Team, by Patrick Lencioni

User Story Mapping: Discover the Whole Story, Build the Right Product, by Jeff Patton

How to Win Friends and Influence People, by Dale Carnegie [I know, but it's genuinely super helpful]

7 Powers: The Foundations of Business Strategy, by Hamilton Helmer

The Lean Startup, by Eric Ries

The Design of Everyday Things, by Don Norman

INDEX

DANIEL THOMASON
PRODUCT LEADER, ECONOMIST & AUTHOR

Daniel Thomason works at the intersection of macroeconomic strategy and high-scale product execution. Currently leading Payments at Google, Daniel oversees the product vision for global Android and Chrome payment ecosystems, driving a future where digital transactions are not only more convenient but more secure and sustainable than old-school plastic cards.

An entrepreneur at heart, Daniel founded Next Level Escape, one of Sydney's most successful and award-winning experiential ventures. This grassroots grit, combined with a decade of tech leadership, is the foundation of his book *All Over It: how to nail your new PM job*, which provides an authoritative guide for the next generation of product managers.

His unique Product Economics approach was forged at Australia's central bank, where he worked as an economist analyzing the financial and payments systems. By applying central bank rigor to digital product ecosystems, Daniel bridges the gap between broad macroeconomic trends and tactical product growth. This rare dual-lens allows him to navigate complex regulatory landscapes and build zero-to-one fintech solutions that scale globally.

Daniel is a sought-after advisor for growing companies and a lecturer on the symbiotic relationship between economic theory and product strategy.